FROM **VICE** TO **VIRTUE**

search: roddegenstein·com
website: roddegenstein author

Written by

~ **ROD DEGENSTEIN** ~

rdegenstein@sasktel
net

From Vice to Virtue
Copyright © 2019 by Rod Degenstein

Tellwell Talent
www.tellwell.ca

ISBN
978-0-2288-0661-5 (Paperback)

Table of Contents

PART ONE
THE DESERT YEARS

PART TWO
NEW LIFE

PART THREE
VICES AND VIRTUES

PART FOUR
THE NARROW PATH TO HOLINESS

Dedications

I would like to dedicate this book to my Mom and Dad, for without them, I would not be here. They were both Roman Catholic and had me baptized as an infant. Baptism! What an unbelievably precious gift! I was so blessed! My parents were my most significant educators. They taught by example. They were hard-working farmers having been raised in Saskatchewan in the first half of the twentieth century. I was raised on a farm and lived in times before there was electricity, telephone or indoor plumbing. Life was good. I always felt secure.

One time I was complaining to my Mom about a friend who seemed to have more than I did. Mom reminded me that I had something that my friend didn't have. I was Roman Catholic. Even as a nine year old, I instinctively knew it was true and I have treasured the value of her response all my life. Another blessing was my Mom's excitement over the apparitions in Medjugorje. Her enthusiasm made my decision spontaneous when I was presented with an opportunity to go. Although my Dad passed away in 1992, he still visits me in my dreams. In addition to dreams, I have felt his hand in many small miraculous events especially with regard to my vehicles.

Acknowledgments

I wish to acknowledge some key people in the writing of my book. When I began over three years ago, I was wondering who my intended audience was going to be. I asked my most trusted friend, Sophie, if she would be part of my practice audience, a role that she has enjoyed ever since. Based on her spiritual depth, I trusted that if she appreciated my work then many other faithful followers might also enjoy it. Her comments have always been encouraging, and sometimes very complimentary.

While in Calgary in the 1990's I had many faith groups to be grateful for. My major ones included the University of Calgary Catholic Community and its prayer group, The Live-In Society, the Calgary Catholic Charismatic Renewal Society, the Medjugorje prayer group and the Calgary Association of Spiritual Exercises Apostolate. They served to root me into my Catholic faith which until then, I knew so little about. There is one last general acknowledgment that I need to include, that being the Lay Formation Program. I began it in Sept. 2015 and will be completing it in June, 2018. It is offered through the Archdiocese of Regina and provides a stimulating, deeply intense, and fulfilling experience for those who wish to deepen their faith. Since I began, it has become the foundation for new spiritual support and growth along with providing inspiring challenges in service and participation. I am being rooted in rich soil which will continue to nourish me long after I finish the program. As I reflect, I feel so blessed by the Lord who gives back a hundred-fold for every small step that I have taken with him. It is impossible for me to express my gratitude to all who have been there to encourage me on my spiritual journey. Telling my story is such a small effort compared to the joy that I have received while on this journey. Thank-you Jesus!

A Bike Ride with Jesus Christ

When I first met Christ
It seemed as though life was rather like a bike ride,
But it was a tandem bike,
And I noticed that Christ
Was in the back seat helping me pedal.

I don't know when it was that
He suggested we change places,
But life has not been the same since.

When I had control, I knew the way,
It was rather boring, but predictable…
It was the shortest distance between two points.

But when He took the lead,
He knew delightful long cuts,
Up mountains, and through rocky places,
At breakneck speeds,
It was all I could to hang on!
Even though it looked like madness,
He said, "Pedal."

I was worried and anxious and asked,
"Where are you taking me?"
He laughed and didn't answer,
And I started to trust.

I forgot my boring life
And entered into the adventure.
And when I'd say, "I'm scared,"
He'd lean back and touch my hand.

He took me to places with gifts that I needed.
Gifts of healing, acceptance, and joy.
He said, "Give the gifts away;
They're extra baggage, too much weight."

So I did, I gave them to people we met,
And I found that in giving, I received,
And still our burden was light.

I did not trust Him, at first, in control of my life.
I thought He'd wreck it;
But He knows bike secrets,
Knows how to bend to take sharp corners,
Knows how to clear high rocks,
Knows how to fly to shorten scary passages.

And I'm learning to shut up
And pedal in the strangest places,
And I'm beginning to enjoy the view
And the cool breeze on my face
With my delightful constant companion, Jesus Christ.

And when I'm sure I just can't do anymore,
He just smiles and says,
"Pedal"

Quoted from <u>Christian-Forum.net</u>

Author's Note

This book is not an autobiography. Instead, it is focused on my personal journey with my Lord and Savior, Jesus Christ, which in some ways is like the bike ride in the previous poem. During any given unit of time, He can show me ecstasy, pain, revelation, and healing, or any other topic that He chooses. It is for me to sort out the events and to put them into themes. My story will not necessarily be chronological because I will be focusing on one theme at a time, with several themes running parallel while on the same time line. It will include personal stories while sharing the lessons that He has taught me. In some places, He challenges me to enhance my learning and understanding. He leads while engaging my heart, mind, and body.

The primary purpose of this book is to give glory to God for all that He has done for me. It is a story of receiving graces, blessings, and crosses along the way. Although the bike ride with Jesus is a good beginning, I talk about "The Way," which is the narrow path that leads to Heaven. I will be referring to virtue and graces that keep us on the right path. I will be referring to the vices, trickery, chaos, and deceit that Satan uses to get us off the narrow path. In my opinion, we are better equipped to do battle with Satan if we have a vocabulary and understanding of his tools and how he uses them. I will also be offering my insights and personal experiences to better prepare the readers for their journey. I am a sinner, having spent more time off the path than on it. It is a daily struggle, and it is only by the grace of God that I can get back on the path and try to stay on it.

There are four sections in my book. The first two definitely are testimonial in nature. The first section is about life when I was trying to control it, with little or no consideration of God. I was living in idolatry, worshiping many false gods including money and pride, and generally being self-centered. As in any testimonial, I would crash and reach rock bottom. I would find myself stripped of everything that I had been taking for granted. Referring back to the poem, I was not aware of pedaling with Jesus. It felt like Hell!

Section two is about the Lord rescuing me and taking me to places that I would never have previously chosen to go. It was a time of spiritual ecstasy. I call it the honeymoon stage of my spiritual journey. It begins in August 1988, and although there are many stages, it never ends. As Thomas Merton, in The Seven Story Mountain, once said, "It is divine in origin and divine in destiny." I know the Lord is rescuing me, his lost sheep, as I learn to listen for His voice and learn to surrender to His will. It is like being a passenger on the bike, with Jesus taking the lead as in the poem above. It is possible only if I live in the grace of God. I continue to this day waiting for my next surprise from the Lord!

Sections three and four are definitely still a part of my bike ride with Jesus and therefore a part of my testimony. However, in these two sections, there is much more emphasis placed on knowledge and beliefs that I have gained while on this journey for almost thirty years. I am not an authority, just an experienced pilgrim with much to learn yet. Everything I have received comes from God, through the Church, its teachings, and members of the Body of Christ. Being a disciple includes many things, especially prayer, study, Scripture, service, and daily reflection. Sections three and four may have some personal opinions that might be imperfect and are therefore in the refining stage. He is the potter, and I am the clay! He is far from being finished with me. Section three ends with a sad conclusion that we, in the Western world, are living in a moral void, or vacuum. It leads into section four with discussions on how we can replace the moral vacuum with holiness as Jesus is calling for us to do.

My background is based on my Roman Catholic faith and from spiritual growth while participating in Catholic charismatic prayer groups, many workshops, and many retreats. I have been to Medjugorje and have belonged to a Marian prayer group. Having done the Spiritual Exercises of St. Ignatius, I have learned about discernment, spiritual direction, and healing. I was involved with RCIA both as a sponsor and as a leader. I have engaged in 12-step programs. I have also participated in personality studies based on Myers-Briggs and the Enneagram. Although I will be making reference to these background experiences, the language in my book should be simple enough for all to understand. It is by the grace of God that I have had these experiences and by His grace that I can share them.

It is my hope that this book will be appreciated by others who recognize that they, too, are on a spiritual journey. Some understanding and appreciation are always enhanced if we can find common ground. Being able to identify with Jesus Christ as Lord and Savior and acknowledging brokenness, a need for spiritual healing, and wanting Christian fellowship make good common ground for those along the way. The ultimate goal is Heaven, and we all need protection from the evil one. There is always a possibility that there may be doubters or skeptics as readers. May the Holy Spirit enlighten and strengthen them as they read about my journey. Remember, I am not the leader, only a grateful witness and pilgrim, and I am writing to give praise and glory to God for all that He has done for me. Come, join me on my journey!

Introduction

In my lifetime, I have made many questionable decisions. Some have been costly, hurtful to others, irreversible, regretful, shameful, and painful. Some have been circumstantial, with few options available, whereas others have been minor, with little or no consequences. Unfortunately, many choices have been mortal and serious enough to cause permanent damage. They were the result of pride, selfishness, and compulsiveness. They have caused me to question my own judgment and ability to make decisions. It is small consolation, but many of these errors are common to all humanity, which encourages me to make myself vulnerable while telling my story.

Experience has caused me to ask questions about destiny and human nature versus cause and effect. Can human nature be changed, or are we all stuck with our own? "It was meant to be" or "It was human nature," or better yet, "The devil made me do it," are examples of not wanting to accept responsibility for our actions. Reflection on the cause and effect of the decision is a more mature way of dealing with it and improves the chances of not repeating the same mistake. I believe that our behavior can be classified as good or bad (virtue or vice) and can be improved.

I will always remember from my early church catechism the answer to the question of our purpose: "Why were we born?" It stated: "We were born to know God, to love God, and to serve Him so that we may someday be happy with Him in Heaven." As a youth, I had a very carefree attitude, perhaps even irresponsible. I trusted that life would unfold as it was meant to, perhaps even believing in a divine destiny. I made many important decisions, such as with marriage, career choices, and house buying, with very little thought or planning. It would be more correct to say that I made decisions by the flip of a coin than to say they had been planned or researched. The reality was that I was miserably unprepared for many life choices, especially marriage. It would be correct to compare myself to a car with one overinflated tire, that being my ego, and three flat tires. I was like an accident looking for a place to crash!

My awareness of my human and spiritual flaws was heightened over thirty years ago when my pride was shattered in the early 1980s. Divorce, obstacles to seeing my children, job and career loss, real estate foreclosures, and bankruptcy were struggles that I had never imagined could happen to me. I experienced all of these losses in three brutal years. They were turbulent and painful. I was in a helpless downward spiral of chaos. My life was not making any sense to me.

My struggles and challenges were on various fronts. With job loss, my financial world and my engineering career were being eroded. My marriage was over, and my relationship with my sons was being challenged with barriers that I had never thought possible. I was dealing with the prospect of eternal damnation, which I feared as a direct consequence of divorce. I felt that I had nowhere to turn and nobody to turn to. I felt alienated and abandoned. Instead of facing my pain and my new situations, I entered into a dysfunctional relationship where denial and alcohol went hand in hand. I would remain in this unhealthy pattern for seven years. I had much to endure while in the desert before the Lord would come to my rescue in August 1988. But praise the Lord! He did come to my rescue. Through my experience, I have a much deeper understanding of suffering and how it relates to redemption. I cannot question suffering except to see it as an invitation to come closer to the Lord.

> *Come to me, all you who are weary and find life burdensome, and I will refresh you. Take my yoke upon your shoulders and learn from me, for I am gentle and humble of heart. Your souls will find rest, for my yoke is easy and my burden light.* (Matthew 11: 28-30)

PART ONE

THE DESERT YEARS

Footprints

One night, a man had a dream. He dreamed he was walking along the beach with the Lord. Across the sky flashed scenes from his life. For each scene, he noticed two sets of footprints in the sand; one belonged to him, and the other to the Lord.

When the last scene of his life flashed before him, he looked back at the footprints in the sand. He noticed that many times along the path of his life, there was only one set of footprints. He also noticed that it happened at the very lowest and saddest times in his life.

This really bothered him, and he questioned the Lord about it. "Lord, you said that once I decided to follow you, you'd walk with me all the way. But I have noticed that during the most troublesome times in my life, there is only one set of footprints. I don't understand why, when I needed you most, you would leave me."

The Lord replied, "My precious, precious child, I love you, and I would never leave you. During your times of trial and suffering, when you see only one set of footprints, it was then that I carried you."

CHAPTER 1

Devastation

When I graduated with a Bachelor of Science degree in civil engineering in 1973, I thought that I had earned a guarantee to a life of success. It was a very proud moment in my life. While in the College of Engineering, we encouraged arrogance, believing that there were two kinds of people: engineers and those who wished they were. It had been a time for parties and nonsense. We worked hard but played even harder. By graduation, we had become very bonded.

I had three offers upon graduation. I began to work in Regina in June 1973 as a sales engineer developing precast concrete contracts. There was much to learn, and my new colleagues were great teachers. I thrived in this industry and in my unique function. I was taking my success totally for granted. Our company was doing well, Western Canada was booming, and my career was flourishing. Besides a company car, an expense account, and bonuses, we also had annual week-long training periods in places like Sunshine Village near Banff or Whistler in BC. My ego was being pumped like never before.

I married in 1975, and in January 1977, I quit my job. Why? My confidence in the future was so positive that I wasn't concerned about taking a break. I purchased an RV and took my wife on a six-month trip as far south as Honduras, spending time in Mexico, Belize, Guatemala, El Salvador, and the Eastern USA. We wanted to start a family but decided to adventure before settling down.

We returned to Saskatchewan in July 1977 and discovered that my wife was pregnant. I found a job in the same precast concrete industry in Vernon, BC. Our two sons were both born in Vernon. Todd was born in 1978, and Dwayne was born in 1979. We decided that Vernon was an ideal place to live while raising a family. However, the company that I worked for started to experience financial difficulty. A friend informed me of an opening with my original company, but this time in Calgary. After further turbulence, I arranged an interview, which was successful. We moved to Calgary where I started my new job on January 1, 1980. Our family began to develop roots in Calgary, where I again was very able to support my family.

Life after graduating from engineering had been good. I had worked hard, always earning a good salary with generous benefits. By mid-1981, I could boast that I had landed a million-dollar contract for each of three companies in each of three provinces. My career resume was excellent. My focus on work had always been intense. However, success in my career had created an imbalance in my family life, which was receiving less focus than required.

Our marriage problems started to become obvious to me only in 1981, and by October that same year, my wife left me, taking our two infant sons with her. In our marriage, I had assumed the role of breadwinner but not best friend. After all, I was an engineer, a fact that I was very proud of. I saw things only from my own perspective, and my wife felt left out of the many family decisions that I had made on our behalf. I had poor communication skills. Expressing feelings was unknown to me. The sad part was that I had no idea what my wife was experiencing. I failed in making her feel cared for. There were enough warnings in 1980 and 1981. In denial, I assumed it was her problem. One of my basic beliefs that kept me in paralysis was that everything would work out. In hindsight, disaster was inevitable. Her attempts to make me understand became reality only after she moved out. Although I was devastated, I coped by entering a state of denial, shock, and numbness. After all, I still had a prestigious job with a company car and a healthy expense account.

In 1981, there were over thirty tower cranes in downtown Calgary. My personal attitude while being challenged with a failing marriage matched the general attitude in Alberta. The entire economy was in boom time, and people were filled with pompousness, arrogance, and a belief that prosperity would continue to escalate. Mortgage rates were around 20 percent, and it was believed by many that they were going to get even higher. How could anything burst this bubble? But a year later, the entire Alberta economy had come to a grinding halt. The thirty tower cranes in downtown Calgary had been reduced to three. The sales volume of the company that I worked for had been reduced to 25 percent of the volume of the previous year. In our industry, there had been enough work to keep four companies scrambling with activity. At first, one major competitor left Calgary, leaving three, which all later struggled to stay afloat. Companies were both letting people go and reducing the working hours for those who were still surviving. Generally, permanent employment with benefits was being replaced by part-time work without benefits. Instead of a readily available staff to process an overabundance of new projects, companies were now hiring consultants to do what little work there was.

In October 1982, 12 months after my wife had left, I lost my prestigious job, which included an expense account and a company car. This loss was different. Divorce was very common in the workplace, where I could hide my pain and shame. But the elimination of a job with benefits left me without work, transportation, and revenue. It was the most devastating one-two knockout punch I have ever received!

There had been warnings. It had been my job to find and develop contracts for our company. Uncertainty was growing like wildfire. Throughout 1982, companies were downsizing and terminating jobs, and confusion became the norm. I knew the inevitable, but I felt helpless. All of Western Canada was going into a downward spiral, with Calgary as the epicenter of the storm. For the most part of the year, I was busy with managing and closing existing files, but nothing new was coming to replace them. I received my notice with a lump-sum severance payment based on being employed with the company for three years, a counseling package to help me re-enter the workforce, and the retention of the company car for three additional months while looking for work.

It was a time of despair. One of my friends had formed a management company a year earlier to capitalize on the boom-time market conditions. I considered that option, but now there was a tremendous pool of very skilled tradespeople without work.

I had thought of applying to a Master of Business Administration (MBA) program. I had been made aware of that career path in 1973 when two of my classmates had entered one. My graduating average from the University of Saskatchewan in 1973 was average. However, with a recent influx of applicants from all over, the University of Calgary had now raised their standards. I would now have to raise my average by taking more classes. If successful at that, I could then enter a waiting line of 700 applicants competing for 70 positions to begin the MBA program. I didn't. Wherever I went, there were lines of displaced professional people. Not only were there unemployed professional engineers, there were accountants, architects, carpenters, and skilled people with management skills from all sub-trades. Terms of employment were changing. People were hired as needed on contractual bases. Other industries, including grocery stores, were changing. They were laying clerks off in order to reduce corporate benefits and hiring part-time help at lower pay and without benefits. This is only a small window of the world in Calgary that I was exposed to when I lost my job in 1982.

My sons and their mom lived near Calgary, so I didn't look beyond Calgary for job replacement. In early 1983, I decided I would try to sell real estate based on my previous experience in marketing and sales. Real estate companies were advertising for realtors. They had little to lose because they did not pay a salary, only commissions after the completion of a transaction. They provided a three-week training program and gave me an office space to work from. I paid to secure a license. Both the competition and market conditions were vicious. The early 1980s were times of high interest (around 20 percent) mortgages and highly inflating property values. Now, in 1983, foreclosures were growing in unprecedented numbers. People were getting desperate. Their mortgages didn't change, but property values were dropping below the value of the mortgage. Add to that a job loss, and it became a potential foreclosure!

From a realtor's point of view, I will share one incident. I had a customer who stopped making mortgage payments immediately after signing the real estate agreement to sell. By the time the property was sold, the selling price had dropped and the debt on the property had risen, both at the expense of the real estate commission. I got nothing! House prices were crashing quickly. I started advising customers to wait because prices would drop even further. The writing was on the wall for me. I would not survive in real estate during this downward spiral.

I lost my first personal property in 1983. After my job loss and before I started selling real estate, I tried my hand at being a landlord. I had added two bedrooms in the basement and had taken in a couple of tenants. But being unemployed, I was unable to meet my financial obligations. The bank, after a ten-month struggle, repossessed my property. By then, I was a realtor, and the number of foreclosures had been escalating. My credit rating had been tarnished, and as a realtor with inside information, I was tempted with an opportunity. I made an offer to purchase a property that had a mortgage worth more than the value of the property. The owner was being transferred to a different province where the real estate market wasn't as severe as in Calgary. In my offer, I requested a healthy cash payment to compensate for the difference between the appraised value and the mortgaged amount, which had an already-high rate of 20 percent. He accepted my offer, escaping from an unfair mortgage, keeping his credit rating intact, and having his corporation transfer him to another location. In addition to purchasing a property without having to apply for a mortgage, my gain was the cash payment plus the real estate commission for representing myself as purchaser and a property to live in. It was located in the same community where I worked as a realtor. I was able to survive for fourteen months, which outlasted my real estate career, before the bank reclaimed the property.

In order to give an example of the changing prices in that era, I will disclose that I had purchased the property for 70 thousand dollars. Two years after the foreclosure was completed, I was invited to the very same property by the new owners. They were pleased because the bank had provided some upgrades and sold it to them for 50 thousand dollars. This was a very typical example of deflation in property values in the early to mid-1980s.

Instead of driving people around as a realtor to show them houses, I began a taxi career. After leasing the cab company's cars and gaining some confidence and experience, I took a further step. I converted my personal car to a taxi in early 1984 and became an owner-operator. One positive thing about driving taxi was that every day was payday. After the loss of my engineering job, my ability to provide maintenance payments had crashed, and so had reasonable access to my children. As a matter of fact, the next three years were very turbulent. I found freedom in driving taxi, but it was only a way of hiding from my financial responsibilities, first and foremost of which were my maintenance payments for child support. The reality was that I had no other option at that time. There were people of all backgrounds in similar positions. Driving taxi was humbling, and I did see humanity from a totally different perspective. I was on the front lines with other suffering human beings, and I was able to hear many individual experiences of the construction crash. The only consolation was that I could now better identify with my parents, who had survived the "Dirty Thirties." I remembered my parents' warnings that it could happen again, but I had dismissed their warnings as old-fashioned rubbish. How wrong I was!

After a second foreclosure, and while driving taxi, I applied for bankruptcy in 1984. It was a nine-month ordeal. The thing that is different about foreclosure and bankruptcy is that the other party is an institution making it black and white and far less emotional than a divorce. The added feature is that you get a fresh start based on a new set of circumstances.

My history of failure on maintenance payments was very significant. There had not been any contingency clauses in my divorce settlement to cover the possibility of less than full employment and, therefore, full support payment. During a period of unemployment and minimal income in real estate, my obligations could not be met. My ex-wife had remarried shortly after leaving me. So, fortunately, the boys had not suffered from financial neglect. However, my greatly reduced economic status created barriers to access to my sons. My ex-wife and I tried different arrangements to compensate for my lack of income. This agonizing period seemed to last forever, but admittedly, it was a very dysfunctional time in my life. I experienced far too much anxiety, grief, and frustration in trying to solve the problem. It is obvious that if two people cannot agree when married, they will never agree when divorced! I knew that I needed help, but my lack of financial resources limited my options. I needed legal advice.

On one occasion, I made an appointment to see a lawyer. He requested two hundred dollars as a binder fee in advance for a consultation, which I begrudgingly paid. After some discussion, he advised me that I was in a power struggle with my ex-wife (as if I didn't know that) and that I should try to work things out with her. He kept my deposit and advised me that he was not interested in representing me. I was starting to realize that being poor was no fun. Powerlessness was a new experience and not one that I would have freely chosen.

I joined a lobby group consisting of other frustrated men with custodial problems. There were many issues, but a common proposal was for joint custody. They believed that the courts were favoring women with child custody and that the rights of men were being ignored or abused. There were many stories of women using their children as hostages to manipulate the father or ex-husband. There were some lawyers who were willing to mediate settlements on behalf of the fathers.

Divine providence was with me. I found the favor of one such lawyer, who was able to deal with my ex-wife very skillfully. Because I was delinquent in maintenance payments, she seemed to hold so much power over me. With his help, I gained a new settlement. My recent bankruptcy had been to my advantage. It acknowledged that I was financially shattered and that I was willing to straighten out my affairs. After all, the courts cared most about the well-being of children and their right to access both parents. My debt to her was minimized, my revised maintenance payments were affordable, and I gained Sunday access. I don't know how many emotional scars my sons and I experienced, but we were now free to have a father-son relationship with fewer unhealthy controlling strings attached. This new arrangement began in the spring of 1985. It felt like a new beginning after three years of financial vulnerability and dysfunctional struggles for access.

In 1985, I also received my annulment from marriage. I had been raised to think that divorce was the worst of all sins and would lead me to eternal damnation. I had been burdened with tremendous guilt since my wife had left almost four years earlier. I didn't know anything about annulments before becoming involved with a support group for divorced Catholics. Their encouragement was consoling but nothing like the relief I felt upon receiving my annulment. I felt forgiven. It was the greatest act of forgiveness that I had ever experienced!

My Catholic faith had always been very important to me. For most of my adult life, I had not been living it very faithfully, but I had roots from my upbringing. With the birth of two sons, I had started to reflect more on religion, and my lack of participation had started to become an issue with me. However, with divorce and the struggles of my past few years, my faith had been put on hold. So, after my renewed access and my annulment, I became very motivated to renew my faith practices. I started taking my two sons to Sunday Mass regularly. I prepared them, and they eventually received their First Communion in 1986.

My sons and I were now able to enjoy a wide variety of activities such as swimming, enjoying the wave pool, batting cages, bicycling, hiking, and summer camping. We enjoyed two weeks of summer holidays, spent at church camps, on trips, or visiting family in Saskatchewan. I was now enjoying activities with my sons that most ordinary families enjoy. The chaos had been replaced with relief. I was able to afford a new lifestyle based on a predictable taxi-driving income. If I needed more money, I could drive more hours.

My new legal settlement, regular access, taking my children to Sunday Mass, and my annulment were all positives. They symbolized an end to a downward spiral that I had been experiencing since my family breakup. They were all helping me move closer to God. There was so much more to unfold before I could start healing, but the period of extreme financial and family devastation was now less critical, and I had regained some stability.

The poem "Footprints" truly applied to these past four years, especially my lack of recognition of His presence. Thank you, Jesus, for carrying me!

CHAPTER 2

Unhealthy Patterns

> *What happens is that I do, not the good that I will, but the evil I do not intend. But if I do what is against my will, it is not I who do it, but sin which dwells in me.*

> (Romans 7:19–20)

Unhealthy patterns can manifest in many ways ranging from a temper tantrum to alcoholic dysfunction. Twelve-step programs and anger management courses have become very available to most North Americans and probably throughout the world. Unfortunately, these patterns, starting as temptations, develop in just about any relationship where there are two parties. It can be between a husband and a wife, a parent and a child, or even in the workplace. Are there common models, and more importantly, are there common solutions?

I have in the past compared myself to a car with one overinflated tire and three flat ones. My overinflated tire was my ego, filled with pride and protected by defensiveness. As already discussed, my world was being shaken in 1982 with divorce, and it was followed by a series of other highly stressful events. I survived by driving taxi in Calgary for five full years.

In addition to my story of devastation, another tragic story would take place. I met a lady after my wife left in 1982. We met at a support group for newly divorced and separated Catholics. I had a haunting fear of eternal damnation for getting a divorce, resulting from fire-and-brimstone preaching during my youth. I found some consolation in learning about annulments and in other people's encouragement that I could get one. Three years later, I would discover the joy of this tremendous act of forgiveness by the Church. This lady seemed to have a lot of knowledge and connections that I needed. I began to trust her as she was instrumental in relieving some of my guilt and shame. Despite being warned about "rebound" by friends, we became very enmeshed far too quickly. She became my confidant, my closest and most trusted friend, and my partner in what would become a highly dysfunctional relationship. She was very persuasive, and I was needy, vulnerable, and gullible because my ego had been fatally wounded. I was clueless, empty, and willing to fall for anything. We developed a pattern of dining and dancing, which provided small comfort in all my confusion. I developed a lifeline of co-dependency on her, which was unhealthy for both of us. As I learned about her life and her pain, I reciprocated by enabling her to become co-dependent on me. The fun that we thought we were having was dampened by irritations, disagreements, and squabbles. We were both on the rebound from broken marriages, and we were both carrying a lot of baggage from the past. We had each other for counselors (the blind leading the blind). I began to compromise on values, being only too willing to cling to the sick romance that we were sharing.

Our state of affairs led to unresolved conflict as we both lacked the required skills. As she developed trust in me, she started telling me more and more horrific stories of her painful past. At first, I enjoyed listening, but it became unbalanced. I felt a duty to listen to her stories. When I tried to assert my own needs, her response was defensive, which caused me to feel guilty. In her opinion, her situation was always far more severe than mine. According to her rhetoric, I was expected to be the strong one. Tensions were building, but she seemed to know when to get us back to the romance stage.

As my tensions were building, they needed to be released. I didn't know any other way except to stuff my feelings. I stuffed them until, finally, we faced a blow-up. For me, it should have been a time to face my reality. I didn't. I felt guilty and blamed myself. Inwardly, I blamed her, but I knew that I would sooner forgive and forget as opposed to not having her in my life. I was locked into a cycle of violence and returned to the aphrodisiac, the romance stage without any resolution. Each time, the romance stage was shorter and less magnetic. The tensions would return with compounding intensity. I knew in my head that this relationship was unhealthy. I still lacked skills for conflict resolution. The time between tension build-ups and blow-ups was shortening. There were long periods of time when we were not together, even for a half-year on one occasion. We both knew that we were not good for each other, but a small spark still existed, and on the few occasions when we did see each other, it ignited so easily, if even for a short time. I desperately needed to end this relationship. Although I tried several times, my efforts were usually dysfunctional, and I felt guilty about my own behavior, which always left me feeling that there was unfinished business. This went on for almost seven years, between 1982 and 1989, which was far too long. I am still embarrassed to admit this, but the power of the patterns that Satan had me stuck in were very powerful, and I was very weak. Diagrammatically, the cycle of violence looks like this, as I learned in a workshop long after mine had ended.

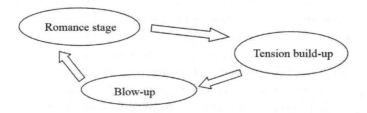

So, how can this cycle be ended? Experts say that the cycle will only end with intervention or when one of the parties finally leaves. Mine ended with intervention. It was both spiritual and miraculous. I will describe some of my miraculous interventions in later chapters, but for now, I simply need to acknowledge that they happened.

One afternoon, much later and after much spiritual transformation, I was able to witness the dynamics of our dysfunctional relationship. I bumped into her in a shopping mall. She invited me to her place. As per previous patterns, she offered me a glass of wine. For the first time ever, I refused. She didn't object. She was going to have one with or without me. I was able to observe her change of personality as she drank approximately four ounces of wine. I was able to excuse myself gracefully and leave. I felt no guilt. Being sober, I was shocked to see the effect that alcohol had on her. Did it have the same effect on me? It made me sick to think that it had. The positive result was that my eyes were opened. I would never let alcohol impair my senses again! Occasionally, I would bump into her but without falling into any patterns. I was free of the cycle of violence!

The whole experience left me with many unanswered questions. Was she an alcoholic? Was I? Never in my life have I craved a drink. I would drink as a result of peer pressure but never because I had no control over drinking. As a matter of fact, since 1989, I have not consumed a large enough quantity of alcohol to make me feel even slightly out of control. I was miraculously delivered from an unhealthy pattern called the cycle of violence and given a distaste for alcohol. Furthermore, I was totally at peace in finally leaving this dysfunctional relationship, but it was only after the Lord's intervention. Thank you, Jesus, for rescuing me!

With my cycle of violence behind me, I was left with many unanswered questions. My search continued well into the honeymoon stage of my spiritual journey. One strategy was to explore the many 12-step programs. After experiencing several different groups and having listened to others' stories, I concluded that I was not an alcoholic. I have never craved alcohol, but I started to realize that I did have an addictive nature. I was a people pleaser, seeking acceptance, hating to confront, and weak in my own convictions. I most easily identified with Co-dependents Anonymous (Coda). I went to meetings regularly and joined study groups. I started doing the steps and working the program.

Twelve-step programs are very spiritual and have a strong basis, coming from Roman Catholicism. I recently discovered an article with a Scripture passage for each of the 12 steps. St. Augustine once said that we are created with an emptiness in our souls that only God can fill. Is it possible that the addicted is in touch with this emptiness and is seeking an aphrodisiac to satisfy the hunger? The aphrodisiac can be alcohol, drugs, sex, or any other substitute for seeking God's help. The result is that we become stuck with enabling, co-dependency, and many other dysfunctional behaviors, which in reality deny our own deep-rooted thirst for God. Only He can fill the emptiness in our souls, and that is how we are created. In the meantime, the world and Satan are having a fire sale on the New Age movement and every other form of false god that they can mold. Jesus said, *"I am the way, and the truth, and the life"* (John 14:5), and it is only this truth that can set us free!

Getting back to the 12-step program, the first three steps are: (1) I can't, (2) God can, (3) let Him. Surrendering to God is a key also for Christianity. Inviting Jesus Christ to be the Lord and Savior of our lives parallels step three of the 12-step programs. The fourth and fifth steps parallel the sacrament of Reconciliation. Step four is to do a fearless inventory of all the hurts we have dealt to ourselves and others, which parallels the examination of conscience in sacramental preparation. Step five is to tell it to another human being, whereas in the sacrament, the confessor tells it to a priest. The sacrament of Reconciliation offers absolution from one's sins and requires that the sinner repent from ever repeating the offense, whereas step six of the program says that the addicted make amends where and when it is safe to do so.

In the evolution of Christianity, Baptism represented salvation. It was thought that ideally, the person would sin no more, but sin was still rooted in human nature, as St. Paul noted. The sacrament of Reconciliation evolved in response to this constant falling from grace of the human. After all, the only difference between a saint and a sinner is that a saint confesses. The Church is said to be "not a museum of saints, but a hospital of sinners."

Unhealthy patterns manifest in different ways, and different support systems have evolved. Anger management courses have become very common due to a need to make a change in one's life in order to stop doing harm to self and to others. Unlike the second step of the program, which is based on self-admission and self-motivation, the courts quite often include anger management as a part of rehabilitation, ignoring the question of self-motivation to make a change or amends.

Another tool for studying unhealthy patterns is the Enneagram. It is a concept based on the supposition that we are all born perfectly balanced. As we develop, we learn to cope but in a familiar way. We continue with this method of coping because it is working for us and we are becoming more confident in this coping mechanism. Compared to other coping skills that are available, we become underdeveloped in other ways and therefore imbalanced. The theory states that there are nine coping methods, or points on a circle. The patterns can be predicted based on this theory or study. As a matter of fact, a path to recovery can be suggested with a surprisingly high level of accuracy, but only after the initial stage of accepting one's imbalance. I found this to be a highly stimulating form of self-discovery, and in addition to participating in three weekend workshops, I read many books and attended regular meetings where others were sharing their experiences based on their preferred method of coping. For those of you who are not familiar with this process, each coping method is given a number. I now realize that these patterns relate directly to virtues and vices. I would like to come back to discuss patterns of vice and virtue based on the Enneagram, but perhaps that could be in my next book.

I learned how to find healthy ways of dealing with my compulsions. I still wrestle with the difference between being compulsive and being spontaneous. My definition suggests that a compulsive action is one without very much thought going into it, whereas a spontaneous action has had previous thought and desire and is followed by a stimulus to act when an opportunity arises. In short, I'm working on being spontaneous without being compulsive.

These above experiences all occurred during the honeymoon stage of my spiritual journey, which I relate in section two of my book. I believe that I was divinely inspired to join in each of the above studies of unhealthy patterns. I was therefore involved in a variety of workshops, book studies, and support groups with lots of personal testimonies by others. My experiences are personal, but my knowledge of the topic is collective and researched. Any knowledge or wisdom that I possess is a gift from God as it is He who has led me into the desert and taught me. Although some of my lessons have been difficult, I also believe that they are to be shared. I'm always challenged by sharing because it is difficult to find an attentive audience. Writing is a way to collect and organize my thoughts while the topic is developing. It is my prayer that if my experiences are divinely inspired, He will continue to use me for the purpose of building His Kingdom and helping others to become free of their bondage to an unhealthy pattern.

CHAPTER 3

Moving Closer to God

I have waited, waited for the Lord,
and He stooped toward me and heard my cry.
He drew me out of the Pit of Destruction,
out of the mud of the swamp;
He set my feet upon a crag; and made firm my steps.
And He put a new song into my mouth, a hymn
to our God.
Many shall look on in awe and trust in the Lord.

(Psalm 40:1–4)

Between 1985 and 1988, I was being drawn closer to God. I had my annulment and regular access, which now included Sunday Mass with my sons at St. John's Parish. I remember driving home after dropping the boys off at 7:30. There was a motivational religious radio show that I would listen to regularly. The closing line was a reminder that "when you draw closer to God, He draws closer to you." It was almost like a Bible study/prayer time, giving closure to the day that I had just enjoyed with my sons.

I had tried unsuccessfully on one or two occasions to read the Bible. I found the Book of Genesis very difficult, if not boring. However, I was getting hungrier for the "Word of God." One of my most memorable experiences was the gift of a Bible. I was talking about my struggles to read the Bible to a perfect stranger, a passenger in my taxi. She actually gave me a Bible, and she suggested that I begin with the Gospel of John. This had to have been divine intervention because it was my 40th birthday! It was not just any day. It was my birthday. It was not just any birthday, but my 40th! The day was May 29, 1988. That biblical number points to 40 years in the desert. What was going to follow would make my first 40 years seem truly like a desert experience. The result was that I completely finished the rest of the New Testament with a passion and desire that only the Holy Spirit can give. Naturally, I went back to the Psalms and Proverbs and continued to read and study. My thirst for Scripture was growing, while my hunger was finding satisfaction.

Seeds were being planted. While driving taxi, I became friends with Sam, an elderly gentleman who loved to talk about the Bible. Our friendship developed, and for over two years, I would visit him, and he would share his favorite Scripture passages with me. Being hungry for the word of God, I was being fed by a taxi customer!

Another noteworthy event happened when a friend of mine from St. John's Parish invited me to a prayer breakfast. I knew nothing of prayer breakfasts, but I trusted her. I started to feel comfortable in this environment after I recognized a few of the nuns who worshiped at St. John's. The guest speaker was Fr. Dave, chaplain from the University of Calgary Catholic Community (UCCC). Listening to a testimonial speaker was new to me, and so were some of the results. He spoke about his life, including his addictions, his pain, and his brokenness. Never before had I heard a priest being so vulnerable. Unknown to me, he was a priest with a 12-step background. I was experiencing emotions as I never had before. During all the horrific losses that I had experienced, I was never aware of sadness, nor did I ever cry. Men are not supposed to cry. The effect of his story on me was that I experienced tears. Previously, I compared myself to a car with three flat tires. My emotional underdevelopment to this stage was one of the flat tires. The few tears I felt were very controlled as usual, but it was a beginning. I did not know how influential he would become while on my spiritual journey. The fact that I was meeting him in this way was so unquestionably divine providence.

Another profound experience of my life was about to take place. In August 1988, I was at a low point. My sons' mom, her husband, and my two sons had moved to Vancouver Island to begin a new life as a family. My regular Sunday visits were over. For three years of Sundays, I had picked the boys up at 10:00, taken them to Mass, and had lunch with them. In the afternoons, we had enjoyed a variety of activities, including movies, playing in a wave pool, swimming, skating, and things that most families enjoy. It was always fun. The evenings were usually sad. After we had supper, I would drive them home by 7:30. However, I always had next weekend to look forward to. For them to move to Vancouver seemed like such a severe loss for them and for me. They were nine and ten years old. I no longer had my two favorite Sunday companions. I felt very alone. However, something was going to happen that would change my life forever.

PART TWO

NEW LIFE

Who among you, if he has a hundred sheep and loses one of them, does not leave the ninety-nine in the wasteland and follow the lost one until he finds it. And when he finds it, he puts it on his shoulders in jubilation. Once arrived home, he invites friends and neighbors in and says to them, "Rejoice with me because I have found my lost sheep." I tell you, there will likewise be more joy in heaven over one repentant sinner than over ninety-nine righteous people who have no need to repent.

(Luke15:4–7)

CHAPTER 4

A Call to Holiness

> *Nicodemus asked Jesus, "How can a man be born again . . . ?" Jesus replied, "I solemnly assure you, no one can enter the kingdom of God without being begotten of water and Spirit."*

> (John 3:4–5)

The expression "born again" is based on this interaction between Jesus and Nicodemus. It is popularly used by charismatic Catholics and evangelical Christians, yet very cautiously used by mainstream Christians. It is understood best by followers who have had a profound conversion experience. It is an experience that is life-changing. It is a spiritual experience that no words can explain. It is etched on the soul, and the memory of it is never lost.

Another scriptural reference comes from John 1: 31, where John the Baptist talks of Jesus and the Holy Spirit: *"The one who sent me to baptize with water told me, 'When you see the Spirit descend and rest on someone, it is he who is to baptize with the Holy Spirit.'"* It appears that Baptism of water and of the Spirit are two different events. I can relate to the above discussion based on my own personal experience.

One night in August 1988, the Lord appeared to me in the shape of a bright shining Communion host. It was 3:00 and still dark, yet His presence lit the room. It was a spiritual experience that I can't explain. There was no noise but an inner voice saying, "Follow me." His presence brought a feeling of total peace and love that I can't describe but that I will never forget. It brought me to my knees in prayer and sobbing with tears of spiritual ecstasy. It was not physically real, but spiritually divine. Ephesians 3:19 says, *"Know the love of Christ that surpasses knowledge, so that you may be filled with all the fullness of God."* This experience surpassed any knowledge of the intellect that I have or ever will have. It was a heartfelt spiritual experience of the love of Christ, which is eternal! I was on fire for the Lord! He had rescued me and put me back on the right path! As I once heard, *"If faith is based on understanding, there are some things which can never be explained. Once you believe, no explanation is required."*

It took future events to realize what had happened to me, and I am still in the process of pondering and reflecting. At first, I thought that an invitation to follow was a single event, but I now see it as an invitation to begin a journey, one that has no end until I am secure with Jesus Christ in Heaven forever!

I saw it as a personal invitation, and it was. My understanding continues to expand, and I now believe that this is one of the great themes of Catholicism. I see life as a spiritual journey and, equally significant, as a call to holiness. God calls us to holiness, and He calls every human being to holiness. A consistent step of being called to holiness is to be set apart. God told the Israelites, *"To me, therefore you shall be holy; for I the Lord am holy, and I have set you apart from other peoples to be my own"* (Leviticus 20:26). St. Paul preached the same message to the Romans: *"Do not conform yourselves to this age"* (12:2). In part four of this book, I expand on the topic of being called to holiness.

Every moment of our lives presents an opportunity to grow in holiness. We are on a spiritual journey, and we are either moving closer to God or we are moving away from Him. Although it appeared as a single spectacular event, it was only the beginning. Many wonderful things that can only be understood as divine intervention or miracles would follow. I was entering the honeymoon stage of my spiritual journey. It was the most exciting time in my life, and it began after being in the desert for 40 years! I was being drawn aside through an invitation to grow in holiness! I was "born again"!

CHAPTER 5

The Honeymoon Stage

He's my Lord, He's my Lord,
He has risen from the dead and He's my Lord
Every knee shall bend, every tongue confess
That Jesus Christ is Lord

After my sons moved, I went to Mass one more time at St. John's, where we had been regularly attending. I opened my Sunday missal only to see their names in it. I was choked. Tears were flowing. I found it too emotional, too lonely without my special companions of three years. I was being called to make a change.

I had been accepted into the College of Education, and I would be starting my practicum year for classroom teaching. So, in September 1988, I began a new leg of the journey. I joined the University of Calgary Catholic Community. The priest was none other than Fr. Dave! I had already been inspired by him when I had gone to my first prayer breakfast. God's intervention is so obvious sometimes, and this was no exception!

I felt welcome immediately. Besides Fr. Dave, there were three other factors that I can share and would recommend for consideration to any parish. Before the procession, we were to <u>exchange greetings</u> with five people. It was new to me, but what a timely ice-breaker. Instead of feeling shy, I felt accepted immediately. Secondly, we were <u>invited around the altar</u> for the Communion Rite. We held hands during the Our Father and hugged during the Exchange of Peace. It was very spiritually intimate and, again, so welcoming. After all, these were all strangers to me. Thirdly, we were <u>invited for coffee and cookies</u> after Mass for fellowship. It was all so different and yet just what I needed. It was a charismatic Mass presided over by a 12-step charismatic Catholic priest! This experience was so refreshing. It was to become a part of my regular spiritual diet.

My love for the Mass as presided over by Fr. Dave was growing. It was a renewed source of grace. I was developing a new understanding of the Mass and its prayers and, yes, even hungering for it. Fr. Dave celebrated Mass twice during the week on campus, so I started going there. Soon after, I started searching out other churches so that I could attend Mass every day. My hunger for attending Mass during the week grew and has remained a constant in my life since 1989. With the benefit of experience and further studies and influences, I more fully understand why I was so drawn to daily Mass. It was instituted by Christ at the Last Supper. The early Christians were not welcome to proclaim Jesus in the synagogues on the Sabbath and were starting to celebrate a meal in personal homes on Sundays. This is referred to in 1 Corinthians 11, written about 56 A.D. The Mass is universal and is celebrated around the world. At any time, on any day, week, or year, Mass is being said somewhere. The prayers of the Mass include the angels and saints, and the whole Christian universe is giving thanks and praise to God in the name of Jesus Christ, our Lord and Savior! And I was unknowingly at the time being drawn closer and deeper into this mystical body, the Church. Praise the Lord!

Fr. Dave preached about healing and 12-step theory. He was able to transform the Gospel into one of mercy and hope for suffering souls like myself. I soon joined their charismatic prayer group, which met regularly on Thursday evenings. It became a regular part of my weekly schedule. In it were many charismatically gifted people, including Fr. Dave and also Fr. Roy, who would soon begin to play an equally significant role in my spiritual growth. At these meetings, in addition to the joyful singing and praising, members were telling their stories of how God had transformed their lives. Healing was a central theme. I was still unfamiliar with healing, but I was developing a deep trust through the testimonials of others.

I started going to retreats, workshops, charismatic prayer breakfasts, and anything that was recommended by my new friends. Remember, I had been in a desert for 40 years and had been so broken and alienated since my divorce seven years earlier. If you've ever been to a bullfight, you might know that they keep the bulls in total darkness before the fight. When they are released, they are blinded by the light. I was in a stage that paralleled these poor bulls, except my colleagues were leading me to and preparing me for the path that Jesus would be leading me on.

As my circle of Christian fellowship continued to expand, I was being asked if I had ever done a "Live-In." It was described to me as being a three-day weekend highlighted with a personal encounter with Jesus. The excitement and faith commitment of the people involved was more than enough to convince me. Whatever they had, I wanted, too. So, late in 1988, I accepted. In February 1989, I did my Live-In. It was the greatest weekend of my life. I do not expect the experience to be matched on this side of Heaven! Considering how damaged I was before attending, it became a weekend of healing. It was filled with charismatic prayer, testimony, and emotion. I was being loved towards wholeness by the Lord. The weekend was filled with surprises, including an altar call. I thought I had died and gone to Heaven!

The weekend was only a beginning. I did not want it to end. I could identify with Peter, James, and John when Jesus was transfigured. They did not want to come off the mountain. I was being taught that the spiritual journey never ends. It continues on to the next event. There were follow-up and support for new members. The Live-In Society was larger than I could imagine. It had been initiated some twenty years earlier by the same Basilian order that both Fr. Dave and Fr. Roy belonged to. They, too, had regular prayer meetings, and it was only natural that I would participate with my newly found zeal. The Live-Ins would continue as long as there were new candidates who were thirsting for the Lord. To paraphrase Jesus: "The harvest was plenty." I actually sponsored several people in the next few years. I was now part of the "back-up," and I worked at least a dozen more retreats over the next three or four years. Each time, I was reminded of my own initial experience, but more importantly, I was inspired by the joy of the new candidates as they shared their encounter with Jesus. Evangelizing was one of the primary purposes of the Live-In, but spiritual fulfillment with all its strengthening, healing, prayer, Bible study, and Christian fellowship was so joyfully evident.

So, after my Live-In weekend, I now had a second prayer group. The two prayer groups were similar, both charismatic, and they complimented each other but had different gifts. The first was for the community, whereas the second, being ecumenical, was for the larger Church body. The gift to me was the same. I felt the love of community and the love of God as I never had before.

Everything had been happening so quickly that I needed time for reflection. Earlier in my honeymoon stage, I had been at a workshop explaining the stages of spiritual development. It had given me a perspective of what was happening to me. In order to better understand our spiritual journey, it is helpful to have milestones along the way. We can use these milestones to discuss where we are and to better understand how they are connected. It also relates to our basic church catechism, which answers the question as to why God made us: "We are born to know God, to love God, and to serve God so that we can be happy with him in Heaven." In order to better understand our journey, we need to reflect regularly on our activities, and what better way than to be as involved as we can be in a community of believers who are also on the journey, which includes workshops and reading.

The speaker classified four stages. The first stage is an <u>awareness that there is a God.</u> We can acknowledge His existence and, yes, say prayers to Him, but in this stage, He is not a personal God. He is a distant God somewhere in the Heavens. We accept Him as a higher power who has created all things, including difficult concepts like eternity. He is someone who has initiated and set the universe in an orderly fashion. We can expand in this stage to learn about our religion and develop disciplines of religious practice. However, everything in this stage is limited to head knowledge.

The second stage is an <u>indirect encounter with the love of God</u> through parents, family, community, especially a community of believers, and any others. It can be very rewarding, and much can be learned about drawing closer to God. I actually experienced the third stage before the second stage, when Jesus personally appeared to me, but it was in the community that I came to understand both stages.

The third stage is <u>to encounter Jesus in a personal way</u> and for us to know and feel how much He loves us. It has a sweetness that cannot be explained, but it provides a spiritual glow that others can sense. Many of the people that I was encountering had been in both stages. All I knew was that I had had my own personal encounter and I was feeling an outpouring of love.

The fourth stage is <u>to move into service</u>, that is, finding a ministry, based on our newly established personal relationship with Jesus. This is easier upon realizing His unconditional love for us. Of course, it goes without saying that one can be at any stage for any length of time and can go back and forth from one stage to another. With the benefit of understanding the journey from the above perspective, I was continuing on my journey of ecstasy.

I previously mentioned Fr. Roy, who was also active with the Live-In Society. He was announcing a pilgrimage to Medjugorje. He called a meeting in October 1988, to tell us about his experiences with a proposal. This would be his fourth pilgrimage there, and he was inviting people to join him. When he showed a video, tears started to flow. I knew I was being called to go! My mother had talked to me about the six children whom Mary had been appearing to since 1981. Although she had been very excited, it seemed to be such a distant and remote place that I hadn't previously considered going. But that night, something changed. Could it be possible that I might be going? After all, the timing was perfect. My university term was ending in April, and the trip was being planned for early May 1989. My uncle had left me a small inheritance, which had enabled me to attend university, and I would have just enough money left for this pilgrimage. So, three weeks later, I committed by signing and making a down payment. There would be sixty of us, with two priests acting as spiritual directors. We started gathering to pray together and to prepare for our venture. On two occasions, we actually rented a bus and went on mini-retreats, praying the rosary and singing hymns to Mary as we journeyed. I was experiencing ecstasy as never before! To put things chronologically, this was happening around the same time as my Live-In experience.

The preparation for the pilgrimage was very stimulating, and my excitement was building. The build-up was small, however, compared to the actual trip and the post-trip experiences that would follow. We left Calgary on the evening of May 2, 1989, stopped briefly in Amsterdam, and then continued to Zagreb, Yugoslavia, where we slept overnight. We traveled by bus to Medjugorje, arriving in time to get settled for the night. Our trip had been filled with excitement, but praying the rosary on the planes and bus was only a prerequisite for our pilgrimage. We slept six nights at our billet and left on the seventh day.

I will always remember our first full day. We went to an English Mass in the morning and a Croatian Mass in the evening. Both times, the Church was packed. In order to get into a pew, you had to slide past those who were exiting until you found a seat. There were five Masses during the day, given in a different language each time. The rosary was prayed at 5:30 in the afternoon during the apparition of our Blessed Mother. The leaders prayed in Croatian, but the response was in many languages, including English, French, Italian, German, Spanish, and others. It made me reflect on the experience of the apostles on Pentecost Sunday and the use of tongues. When the Blessed Mother appeared, the entire church became absolutely silent. The children were listening and interacting with the Virgin Mary, and the entire congregation was entranced. The spiritual feeling that I experienced and witnessed was indescribable. Although her appearance was short, the reverence that followed was divine.

Needless to say, my first day was prayerful. Aside from two Masses and the Sacrament of Reconciliation, I had participated in praying the rosary seven times. I had actually taught a young lady from our group to pray the rosary. The next few days were equally prayerful. We spent time praying the rosary on Apparition Hill and on the Hill of the Cross, where we also did the Stations of the Cross. There was much excitement resulting from the happenings and miracles of the pilgrims.

I hit a low on the sixth day. We were going to visit Fr. Yozo's church. He had been the resident priest at St. James when the children had started seeing Mary in 1981. Fr. Yozo was doing a healing Mass for the pilgrims. Many were being slain in the Spirit, which is a term used to describe a deepened spiritual ecstasy. Although half of our group from Calgary had the experience, I didn't. It was time for my pity party!

With eight months of a fairly intense charismatic background, I wasn't accustomed to having Mary play such a significant role as she was receiving in Medjugorje. I was being emotional, not rational. Being slain in the Spirit is associated with charismatic spirituality more than Marian. So, what was this all about? I didn't try to reason; I simply felt. I was doubting the value of being there. I was in desolation. It was like the darkness before the light. Fortunately, I didn't remain in that state for very long.

Early next morning, I was doing the Stations of the Cross on Krejavic Hill. The meditation for the tenth station was telling us how important it is to Jesus that we accept Mary as His mother and that we honor her for her relationship to

Him as Mother of God and as Mother of the Church. The message was one of conviction, and I was being scolded by the Lord. I admitted my guilt. As a matter of fact, I confessed in the sacrament of Reconciliation later that day. For now, I had to deal with tears as I could feel them coming. This took place before breakfast. This was going to be our last meal with our billets, who had treated us royally.

During breakfast, the hostess gave me a statue of Mary. There were ten of us in her house, and I was the only one to receive a gift from her. I understood the connection. It was only earlier that day that I had accepted Mary as my mother, and somehow, the hostess knew that something divinely special had happened. I started to cry. We walked to Mass. Friends were passing me Kleenex. I sobbed uncontrollably all through Mass. Only yesterday, I had doubted the value of being in Medjugorje, and today I was falling apart because we had to leave. Yet I felt joy because I knew that I was receiving grace as I had never before experienced! Instead of being slain in the Spirit the day before, I was now in a state of joyful ecstasy, and I would return to this joyful state daily for at least another three or four months, always with tears and sobbing. It was an intense time of healing. I will dedicate another chapter to healing later in my book.

The days after our pilgrimage were very fruitful. I was now attending daily Mass along with tears of joy and gratitude. Medjugorje was in my heart, my conversation, and my music. Many in our group were very bonded to each other. We always had a function to attend, and we were joyful to see each other. We formed a prayer group to share our experiences and to offer each other support and encouragement. What had happened and was continuing to happen was real. Other people who later went to Medjugorje joined our group. I participated regularly, once a month, until

I left Calgary in 2002. As far as I know, they continue to meet. My honeymoon stage continued, but it led to another special event, which I will now isolate and relate in the next chapter.

CHAPTER 6

My Own Eucharistic Miracle

I announced your justice in the vast assembly;
I did not restrain my lips, as you, O Lord, know.

(Psalm 40:10)

Shortly after Medjugorje, I went to a workshop on ecumenism. The main purpose was to find common ground and to break down barriers among the various Christian denominations. There were about 80 people in attendance, and we randomly formed ten groups of eight.

The question was posed: "What is the biggest obstacle to unity amongst the Christian churches?" One of the groups cited the belief of the true presence in the Eucharist. They said that some Christians find it only symbolic. It becomes special because it is the focus of everyone's attention at that time of the service. They compared it to sunlight coming through a magnifying glass. With enough concentration of sunlight, a fire could start. They were suggesting that the people's focus was the source of power!

I was in disbelief, and without any hesitation, I raised my hand, stood up, and recited the story of the Miracle of Lanciano. In the 800s there was a priest having a crisis of faith. He was doubting the true presence in the Eucharist, but as he elevated the host during the consecration, he could feel a transformation in the Host. After elevating the chalice, he noticed that the wine had changed to blood. He now totally believed! Because his experience was so profound, they preserved the Body and Blood of our Lord in the exact state following consecration until around the 1970s. Based on modern technology, and believing that it could be proven, the bishop allowed an investigation. The blood had remained incorruptible for 1200 years, and the Host proved to be not only flesh but that of a crucified heart. I finished my story of Lanciano with the conclusion that there are certain things that cannot be compromised nor explained but must be accepted as mystery!

During the lunch that followed, I received a variety of comments from others that caused me some uncertainty. Had there really been such a miracle? Should I have told about it? Had I sabotaged some progress towards unity?

My doubts were erased a few days later. I dreamed that I was with Jesus as He was distributing the fish and the loaves. After the loaves were distributed, He turned to me with a look of frustration on His face. He said, "You know, Rod, people can accept that I am both God and man. So why can't they accept the fact that I am Body, Blood, Soul, and Divinity in the Eucharist?" I'll never forget that consoling, comforting, and oh so personal experience in such a blessed dream with Jesus being so personal with me!

As I reflect on that topic, I have come to appreciate John 6:51: *"I myself am the living bread come down from heaven. If anyone eats this bread he shall live forever; the bread I will give is my flesh, for the life of the world.*" Jesus is describing Himself as the bread of life. He tells us that we must eat His body and drink His blood in order to have eternal life. Many followers either could not understand or could not accept His teaching, so they left. I fear for our many brethren because there still seems to be much doubt about the true presence even today.

I have never been to Lanciano, and in the last twenty-five years, I have met fewer than five people who have. Recently, I met a priest who had been there. He confirmed my story and added that the blood type is the same as on the Shroud of Turin and as in other Eucharistic miracles that have been investigated, including one by our current Pope Francis when he was a cardinal. Their stories confirm the miracle. But now I have my own, my personal dream with Jesus during the multiplication of the fish and the loaves and the true presence in the Eucharist. I feel so blessed, not so much by my consoling dream, but by the fact that Jesus loves us so much and wants to be with us always. He instituted the Eucharist on the first Holy Thursday knowing that He would physically depart but that His kingdom had come and would remain. Mass is being celebrated somewhere in the world at any given time, and the Blessed Sacrament is present in the tabernacles around the world. We are so blessed to have such an awesome God who is constantly reaching out wanting and waiting for us to come to Him. This miracle story has permanently etched my soul, and the Eucharist remains ever so precious. Thank you, Jesus!

CHAPTER 7

The Honeymoon Shifts

I remained very active on my journey. After all, I had three faith communities, daily Mass, Scripture studies, and lots of Christian fellowship. Believing that the Lord had been preparing me for something, I started to think about a call to the priesthood. When invited for a weekend on vocational discernment by Fr. Dave, I went along with two other young men. "Many are called, but few are chosen" (Matthew 22:14). Eventually, one of the three of us did become a priest. The reality was that I was still too broken and needed to encounter much more healing. This truth only became evident with the benefit of hindsight.

I was planning another pilgrimage to Medjugorje in 1990. I was savoring my previous experiences, and I was wanting more. However, the Lord had other plans for me. I was going to enter into two other major areas that were unfamiliar to me. They are so very connected to each other that they need to be introduced together. It would not be correct to say that I was leaving my honeymoon stage, because I was still going to experience much joy and I would know that I was still delightfully being held in the arms of the Lord. I was going to get involved with the spiritual exercises and, along with them, healing. I have already mentioned healing because I believe that tears are simply God's way of washing our damaged souls. I will continue by referring to a couple of passages from Scripture on healing before getting to my initiation to the exercises.

> *Jesus and the disciples came to Bethsaida. Some people brought to Jesus a man who was blind and begged Jesus to touch him. Jesus took the man who was blind, by the hand and led him out of the village; and when he put saliva on his eyes and laid his hands on him, he asked him, "Can you see anything?" And the man looked up and said, "I can see people, but they look like trees, walking." Then Jesus laid his hands on his eyes again; and the man looked intently and his sight was restored, and he saw everything clearly. Then Jesus sent the man away to his home, saying, "Do not even go into the village."*

(Mark 8:22–26)

My experiences of healing until now have been based on uncontrollable sobbing and without any rational explanation. Certainly, they were not connected to any one certain event or any singular issue. They had been of the extraordinary, spontaneous type, as are most of the healing stories by Jesus in Scripture. Why then this Scripture passage? It introduces the topic of progressive healing, which means that healing can take place over a period of time. Life, too, is filled with both extraordinary and progressive events. For example, a couple wants a baby. There are many events that precede the birth of the child. When the baby is born and cries its first cry, the event becomes extraordinary. There are few experiences as exhilarating as the birth of a child. The events that preceded and that follow are not as extraordinary, but they are all connected. The above passage supports the reality that most healing is ordinary and is sometimes likened to the peeling away of the layers of an onion.

> *Having heard this he called loudly, "Lazarus, come out!" The dead man came out, bound hand and foot with linen strips, his face wrapped in a cloth. "Untie him," Jesus said, "and let him go free."*

(John 11:43–44)

There is another element to healing. Jesus resurrected Lazarus from the dead. He clearly wants us to unbind each other. Any communal gathering such as Mass, prayer groups, 12-step meetings, funerals, and many others are examples where people help to heal each other. So, yes, Jesus is the ultimate healer, but he is asking us to love each other and to be involved in the healing process.

I was starting to observe how the Lord was directing me. I started to see coincidental events as divinely directed. I had already felt His hand upon me, but now it was becoming more frequent and more obvious to me. I was beginning to watch for Him, desiring to meet him in another unexpected event. On one occasion, at Mass on a Sunday, I noticed a brochure that had been left behind announcing a workshop on dreams for the following Tuesday. It seemed personal. Not only had it been left in the pew that I'd chosen to sit in, but I had already been booked for substitute teaching for the other four days of the week. I smiled and said, "Lord, if you want me to go to the workshop, keep the day open for me." He did. I went. Fruits of the experience followed.

Shortly after the workshop on dreams, I dreamed of my dad. He was a farmer who loved animals. Whenever I went home, he would be waiting to show me any new life on the farm. In my dream, Dad was telling me that he had a new horse for me to ride. I, too, loved horses, and I was excited to share his excitement. We were walking to the barn, and I began to choke. In my dream, I was having an asthma attack. It was traumatic enough to wake me and end my dream.

As I awoke, streams of tears were rolling down my face. In reality, I could not live on a farm. I was an asthmatic, and at a very young age, my health was a concern. Barns with grain dust in them were quite often a trigger. The dream reminded me of my lack of being engaged in activities that my dad loved. At a subconscious level, I was grieving the separation from my dad after I left home at the age of 18, although my visits back to the farm were many. These tears were also joyful but specific for my dad. The dream showed me the unconditional love that my dad had for me. It was profound. My dad passed away shortly after, and I still dream of him. In my dreams, he is still a loving, caring father. Far too often, I have had life experiences outside of dreams that have convinced me that my dad is still protecting me.

I'd already been engaged in the exercises when I had this dream experience. Keeping a journal is common to both the exercises and dream analysis. As I wrote about my dream, I wept. As a matter of fact, I shared my dream experience three or four times with friends, and each time, I would weep. I was having a healing experience. This, for me, was an example of how others can support us in healing. Trusted people can provide a safe place to enable our healing just by respectfully listening. This is our way of accepting Jesus's invitation to "unbind him" as He did for Lazarus. Keeping a journal and reflection help me to see the awesomeness of God in my life.

Thank you, Jesus, for arranging for me to go to a workshop on dreams! And for the closeness to my dad in dreams and in the events of daily living!

I want to tell one story that I consider to be of divine providence, and you can be the judge. My dad passed on December 2, 1992. I wanted to stay with Mom, newly widowed, over the Christmas and New Year season, which I did. I lived in Calgary at the time, and it was a 10-hour drive to Mom's home in Saskatchewan. I rarely look under the hood of a vehicle; some would call me irresponsible. On this particular day, I was packed and ready for a 10-hour drive to stay with Mom. Before I started the vehicle, I thought I would check under the hood. To my dismay, I discovered that my fan belt was missing. I was grateful that I had not had a problem the day before. Discovering that I could have it repaired promptly, I left it at a service station, had breakfast at a nearby restaurant, and was on my way. I immediately gave credit to the Lord for the timing of a problem that could have resulted in much greater grief had I not been in touch with the prodding of the Holy Spirit. Adding this story to others relating to vehicles has deepened my belief that my dad is still looking after me!

CHAPTER 8

Discernment and the Spiritual Exercises

In my honeymoon stage, I had already been introduced to discernment from a workshop that I had enjoyed. Discernment is an understanding in decision making. Is the decision to be made based on the will of God, or is it based on some other voice? The speaker outlined four voices at work in our decision making: the Holy Spirit, peer pressure, patterns, and Satan.

The first voice is the <u>Holy Spirit of God.</u> John10:14 states: *"I am the good shepherd. I know my sheep and my sheep know me."* When He speaks to us, we simply know. We can also judge by the fruits of the Spirit. It helps if we know virtues (versus vices), right (versus wrong), and good (versus evil). We need to understand the opposites for discernment. The term the Church uses for knowing right from wrong is "an informed conscience."

The second voice is that which results from <u>peer pressure.</u> Peer pressure in itself is not good or bad. Following good examples is a positive application of peer pressure. However, there are many distractions that come from others giving a negative influence. Peer pressure needs discernment, a process that helps us to know whether our decision is moving us closer to God (grace) or pulling us away from God (vice). Secularism and relativism are two big examples that are pulling the Western world away from God.

The third voice in discernment is based on <u>patterns</u>. Patterns are developed and are not seen as serious, yet they can be so damaging to oneself and to relationships with others. Following this workshop on discernment, I would gain extensive experience with both 12-step programs and the Enneagram, as I previously discussed in Chapter 2.

The fourth voice is that of <u>Satan</u>, the deceiver. He is the "Father of Lies." We need to understand vices (deadly sins) and techniques of manipulation, coercion, exploitation, control, and every mind game that is possible. Satan is constantly lurking and is capable of causing much chaos and darkness wherever and whenever he is allowed.

Most mature adults have a clear perception of the Holy Spirit versus Satan. Peer pressure and patterns are much more difficult to see. I believe that Satan masterfully uses these two voices to get us onto the slippery slope where we think we have control but where we have compromised enough to have lost balance unknowingly. Then we slip and slide until something far more serious happens. The topic of the slippery slope continues in Chapter 19.

The above theory about the four voices was given to me at a workshop that the Lord had directed me to. It serves as basic introduction to discernment, but the Spiritual Exercises of St. Ignatius take us much further. Now I will relate how the Lord worked to get me doing these exercises. As already discussed, in my honeymoon stage, many things were happening to me that I would relate in my various prayer groups. People recognized my zeal for the Lord. I was asked a couple of times if I had ever heard of or done the Spiritual Exercises of St. Ignatius. My response was that they were unfamiliar to me, and besides, I was planning a second pilgrimage to Medjugorje with the same church group. As the time for making the down payment for the trip grew closer, I started to think that the Lord did, perhaps, have a different plan for me.

I had become undisciplined with waking up in the morning. I was a substitute teacher, and I wasn't guaranteed work every day. I began to sleep a little longer on days when I didn't get called to work. Being dissatisfied with my attitude, I decided to set an alarm for 7:30, asking the Lord if that time was okay. If not, what time would He want me to awake? It was too coincidental to be anything but divine. The telephone rang and rang only once. It was exactly 6:30 in the morning, not a minute before nor after, but exactly 6:30! I accepted it as an answer to prayer. It would become a discipline in order to do the exercises that I was being prepared for but without my knowledge of things to come!

Very shortly after, at a prayer meeting, a blind friend asked me to open a letter addressed to him and to read it. It was from the Calgary Association of Spiritual Exercises Apostolate (CASEA). He asked me if I wanted to do the exercises. There were three other spiritual directors at this prayer meeting, unknown to me at that time, but with the benefit of hindsight, they seemed to already know that I would be starting. The Lord had already convinced me to wake at 6:30 for prayer. I knew that the exercises were to take an hour every day, and so it became rather clear that the Lord was calling me. They informed me that there was a discernment period and that together with a director, a final decision could be made. The exercises could take a full year. Although it was a major commitment, I accepted the invitation. Instead of going to Medjugorje for the second time, I began the Spiritual Exercises of St. Ignatius.

The form of prayer was meditative based on a given Scripture passage. We were to apply all of our senses, putting ourselves into the passage, and to see, hear, smell, taste, and touch anything that might be happening. We were to remain focused on the reading and eventually to dialogue with Jesus. Based on the insights from the experience, we were to pray to Him. My experiences in my prayer time were quite profound. Together with my director, after two months, we agreed that I was called to do the actual exercises.

What are spiritual exercises? St. Ignatius wrote: "The purpose is to prepare and dispose the soul to rid itself of all the disordered tendencies. After it is rid, to seek and find the Divine Will as to the management of one's life for the salvation of the soul" (*Spiritual Exercises*, year, page number).

As I got deeper into the spiritual exercises, I developed a vocabulary of new terms: consolation, desolation, detachment, poverty of spirit, virtues, and vices. My director gave me a chart showing the seven deadly sins (vices) and how they matched with the seven virtues. The picture that my director gave me became permanently etched in my mind. I always thought that if I were to ever write a book, it would be on the movement of the Spirit "from vice to virtue," hence the title of my book.

I completed the exercises in about 18 calendar months, which included summer breaks. The discipline of morning prayer was rewarding, as spending time with the Lord should be. I would be sad when they were finished, but unknown to me, there was follow-up. There were more courses and workshops as next steps, which would eventually train me to become a spiritual director. I was introduced to both the Myers-Briggs Type Indicator (MBTI) and the Enneagram. I was very passionate about both and participated in several workshops deepening my understanding of both.

The concept of the Enneagram is based on the supposition that we are all born in perfect balance. There are a number of ways to cope with stress, but as we grow older, we develop a unique way. The more familiar we become with it, the stronger we become in that way of coping. However, there are other ways of coping, and we seem to miss out on those because we become dependent on our preferred method. As a result, we become imbalanced or even eccentric with many resulting blind spots. One purpose of the Enneagram is to heal from unhealthy patterns, which I have previously discussed.

The theory states that there are nine points. Each point has a vice and a virtue with a stress and relaxation movement associated with it. The stress movement becomes an unhealthy pattern if allowed to go unchecked. The relaxation movement, when chosen through discernment, leads to healthiness. I was able to see my own imbalance and how the Lord was leading me to wholeness. This could lead to a very lengthy discussion, but I will discuss the Enneagram only as it relates to the exercises.

I discovered a divine connection between the movements in the Enneagram and the spiritual exercises. My spiritual director had given me a table on vices, virtues, and false virtues. When I discovered the parallel, I was in absolute awe. God works in such mysterious ways. He gave the Enneagram to the Muslims (the Sufis) who protected it for centuries before the Western world gained access to it less than two hundred years ago. It was St. Ignatius, founder of the Jesuits, who developed the spiritual exercises in the 1500s.

It was this connection between the two that became my final motivation for writing my book. It seems to be appropriate, as I have just done, to introduce the concept of the Enneagram before moving on to the next section. I will choose to leave my own self-revelations from the Enneagram for another book. The next section is about vices and virtues based on Church teachings, with some personal reflections and experiences. I will be switching from an emphasis on personal story to more about related knowledge that I have gained while on this wonderful journey. Most of the information in the next two sections is the result of recent study and retention from previous workshops.

It is also noteworthy that I completed the studies to become a spiritual director in 1994. I was a member of CASEA for a year. I was entrusted with a person to direct. My association with CASEA ended when I experienced illness in 1995. I was forced to re-evaluate my personal activities. I also dropped two other commitments, both relating to Church but not to vices and virtues. The Lord was causing me to change directions. He wanted to give me some teaching experience. He is the potter, and I am the clay.

> *I went down to the potter's house and there he was working at the wheel. Whenever the object of clay which he was making turned out in his hand, he tried again, making of the clay another object of whatever sort he pleased. Then the word of the Lord came to me: "Can I not do to you, house of Israel, as the potter has done?" says the Lord. "Indeed like clay in the hand of the potter, so are you in my hand, house of Israel."*

(Jeremiah 18:3–6)

PART THREE

VICES AND VIRTUES

From Mount Hor they set out on the Red Sea road, to bypass the land of Edom. but with their patience worn out by the journey, the people complained against God and Moses. "Why have you brought us up from Egypt to die in this desert, where there is no food or water? We are disgusted with this wretched food!"

In punishment, the Lord sent among the people sariph serpents, which bit the people so that many of them died. Then the people came to Moses and said, "We have sinned in complaining against the Lord and you. Pray the Lord to take the serpents from us." So Moses prayed for the people, and the Lord said to Moses, "Make a seraph and mount it on a pole, and if anyone who has been bitten looks at it, he will recover." Moses accordingly made a bronze serpent and mounted it on a pole, and whenever anyone who had been bitten by a serpent looked at the bronze serpent, he recovered.

(Numbers 21:4–9)

CHAPTER 9

Vices and Virtues

When Moses lifted up the serpent, the people who gazed on it saw two things. They got a look at their own sins, and they could see how the serpent (Satan) slithers amongst people. Sin is deadly, and it interferes with how God would like to take care of His people as He had been doing for the Israelite before they started to complain. Secondly, they got a look at God's mercy. Whoever looked at the bronze serpent was instantly healed!

This reading from circa 1350 B.C. points the way to looking at sin, which makes the need for healing. The pole is symbolic of the Cross and our sins. If it points to sin, it also points to the sacrament of Reconciliation, which Mother Church, through the direction of the Holy Spirit, instituted for us. Just as the Israelites needed to look at their sins for healing, so must we. When we look at our sins and confess them, something divine happens. We receive forgiveness and divine mercy, a greater form of healing than any psychologist can provide!

Remember, as previously discussed, the spiritual exercises also require that we reflect on our sinful nature. Yes, it is worth repeating. Remember, "we are to prepare and to dispose our soul to rid itself of all the disordered tendencies." And again, the second part of the exercises is "to seek and to find the Divine Will as to the management of one's life for the Salvation of the soul." Does this also not resemble very closely the two sacraments of Reconciliation and Eucharist?

I have already introduced these two great gifts of the Church (Reconciliation and the spiritual exercises), so let's begin a discussion on vices and virtues. The Church has helped us to understand sin and how it affects our relationship with God. From Proverbs 6:16–19: *"There are six things that the Lord hates, yes seven are an abomination to him; haughty eyes, a lying tongue, and hands that shed innocent blood; a heart that plots wicked schemes, feet that run swiftly to evil, the false witness who utters lies, and he who sows discord among brothers."*

As early as 500 AD, Pope Gregory had revised a couple of earlier lists to form the more common seven deadly sins. They were listed as lust, gluttony, greed, sloth, wrath, envy, and pride. Although there are more than seven virtues, the Catholic Church has recognized seven capital virtues as opposites to the seven sins. According to Dante's *The Divine Comedy*, (around 1300 AD), the sins have an order of greatness, and the virtues a respective order of greatness as well. This order is shown from the lowest to the highest.

VICES	VIRTUE
Lust (excessive sexual appetite)	Chastity (purity)
Gluttony (overindulgence)	Temperance (self-restraint)
Greed (avarice)	Generosity
Sloth (laziness/idleness)	Diligence (zeal/labor)
Wrath (anger)	Patience (meekness)
Envy (jealousy)	Brotherly Love (kindness)
Pride (vanity)	Humility (humbleness)

The sins (vices) can be simply defined, again, in the same order:

1. Lust is an inordinate craving for the pleasures of the body.
2. Gluttony is an inordinate craving to consume more than one requires.
3. Greed is the desire for material wealth or gain, ignoring the realm of the spiritual.
4. Sloth is the avoidance of physical or spiritual work.
5. Wrath is manifested in the individual who spurns love and opts instead for fury.
6. Envy is the desire for another's traits, status, abilities, or situation.
7. Pride is the excessive belief in one's own abilities, that interferes with one's recognition of the grace of God. It has been called the sin from which all others arise. It is also known as vanity.

The Church has much to say about virtue. One of my sources from Wikipedia said that there are 52 virtues mentioned in Scripture. Some of these virtues have common ground and can, therefore, be classified. Some are more divine in nature, whereas others can be developed by all humans. The first major classification is that of the theological virtues, which are faith, hope, and love. They are totally free gifts that cannot be earned but are received through sanctifying grace. They are dispositions of the heart. The apostle Thomas, in his doubting, exemplifies Faith. John 20:25 states: "*His answer was 'I will never believe it, without…'*"Then, a week later, when Jesus appeared again to the apostles, this time with Thomas present, "*Thomas said in response, 'My Lord and my God!'*"

(John 20:28) This expression of faith was clearly a change of heart based on Grace.

St. Augustine once said that if we try to understand before we believe, there are always going to be things that we cannot understand. But if we believe, then no explanation is necessary. Although the feast day of the Assumption of the Blessed Mother into Heaven is such an example, it is more about hope. We as Christians in faith believe in Heaven and an afterlife, but this feast day gives us hope that our mortal bodies will one day be perfected in glory and will be present with our Lord and Savior in Heaven for all eternity! That kind of hope is truly a gift of sanctifying grace.

The love of God is like the air that we breathe. There is such an abundance that we can never use all of it, yet it can be polluted. In parallel, the love of God can be polluted by sin. Like any gift, we can lose it if we don't properly cherish and nurture it. These gifts are to be shared. As pointed out in 1 John 4:7: *"Beloved, let us love one another because love is of God; everyone who loves is begotten of God and has knowledge of God."*

Another classification is that of the cardinal virtues, which can be developed and practiced by anyone. They are habit forming and, by grace, have the firm disposition to do good. They are both the outgrowth of habit and sanctifying grace. Therefore, they may take on both a natural and supernatural dimension. They may grow to perfection in faith and as the fruit of our own good work. The four cardinal virtues are as follows:

1. Prudence is the ability to distinguish what is good from bad or right from wrong. It deals with the intellect.
2. Justice deals with the will. It demands that we deal with fairness to all parties concerned.

3. <u>Fortitude</u> (courage) allows us to overcome our fears and to continue in our Christian tasks.
4. <u>Temperance</u> is concerned with our restraint and moderation of our desires for food, sex, pleasure, and drink. It deals with the will.

The seven capital virtues have already been listed above and will be discussed further with their contrast to the seven deadly sins. They are similar to the cardinal virtues in the sense that they are the outgrowth of habit and a disposition to do good. However, they differ from the cardinal virtues in the sense that they are more for the purposes of overcoming the seven deadly sins.

So, by the grace of God and by our own good works, which dispose our soul to His grace, it is possible to grow in virtue. In the chapters ahead, we will be comparing not only vice to virtue but the inclusion of a false virtue. We can compare our actions as they go from vice to virtue and then on to a false virtue to a pendulum swing. If the center is the virtue and vice is the extreme swing, then the swing to the other side is the false virtue, or simply another vice. The challenge in discernment is to know the virtue and to cling to it instead of swinging to another vice. It is true that vices are all related and interconnected because they are all steps in moving away from a right relationship with God. Similarly, virtues are all related and interconnected because they are tools for maintaining a right relationship with God. The discussions ahead will be based on the seven capital virtues and how they offset the seven deadly sins and any false virtues that Satan may try to disguise to camouflage a virtue.

If a pendulum is symbolic of hypnosis, then Satan uses it masterfully to prevent us from being virtuous and keeping us on the narrow path that leads to Heaven. O how we need a Savior! Hopefully, after a review of some of the vices and virtues, we will be better able to see our own fallen nature and to face it as the Israelites did when they put the serpent on the pole. Hopefully, when we do our part, we will grow in experiencing God's mercy and strengthen our resolve to grow in right relationship with God and neighbor.

Prayer to St. Michael

St. Michael the Archangel, defend us in battle. Be our protection against the wickedness and the snares of the Devil. May God rebuke him, we humbly pray and do thou, O Prince of the Heavenly hosts, by the Divine power of God, cast into Hell, Satan and all the evil spirits who prowl through the world seeking the ruin of souls. Amen.

Pope Leo XIII

CHAPTER 10

From Pride to Humility

The beginning of pride is man's stubbornness in withdrawing his heart from his Maker.

(Sirach 11:12)

Lucifer thought that he was the most beautiful angel in Paradise. In his state of self-admiration and pride, he forgot that he was a creature, denying that his beauty was a gift from God. Indeed, in his state of pride, he wanted to compete with God. The result for Lucifer was his fall from Heaven and his transformation to Satan.

Pride has been said to be the greatest of the seven deadly sins. It is the basic belief that one is essentially better than others, the failure to acknowledge the accomplishments of others, and excessive admiration of the personal self (especially holding self out of proper position towards God). It is a refusal to acknowledge the role that God has played in our good fortune. Competitiveness by itself is not a bad quality, but it is a characteristic of a proud person, so a desire for power and control may follow, leading to lust and avarice.

My pride was most obnoxious when I graduated with a civil engineering degree in 1973. I was convinced that there were two kinds of people in the world: those who were engineers and those who wanted to be. I was moving further and further from God. My ego was totally inflated, and I was blinded by my recent success. The reality was that if I had been a car, I would have had three flat tires and one overinflated one. Most cars would crash, and so did I, as I have described in earlier chapters.

Other vices that follow pride are shame and guilt. When my marriage failed, I started to experience shame. I was a failure! I was in denial. I had made a mistake, but without understanding humility, I didn't realize that I was as precious in God's eyes as ever before. After the divorce, I felt extremely guilty. I was convinced that I was going to go to Hell for eternity! Failure in family was the result of pride, and now the two demons of guilt and shame were taking their turns at beating me!

Humility is having a clear perspective, and therefore respect, for a right relationship with God. All good things that we have are gifts from God. He is the Giver, and we are the receiver. The word "humus" means rooted and, in this case, rooted in the truth of who we are, that is, creatures of God but not gods. In humility, we are also rooted in the truth of our uniqueness and specialness. There is no other being like yourself. However, there is a divine purpose to our unique creation, and we must always remember, as Mary did, that we are to do God's will.

Luke 1:38 states: *"Mary said, 'I am the servant of the Lord. Let it be done to me as you say.'"* Our Mother Mary is a model of humility. She said yes at the Annunciation. She was willing to trust that God had a unique plan and role for her to play in salvation history. I have been praying the rosary regularly since my pilgrimage to Medjugorje almost thirty years ago. The first decade of the joyful mysteries is for the intention of the grace of humility. As I grow in humility, it is easier to recognize when I have slipped off the narrow path and easier to reconcile in order to get back to a right relationship with God. It is becoming easier to give credit where credit is due to my Lord and Savior Jesus Christ!

Scripture talks about the narrow path. Virtues are on the narrow path, and the devil is always lurking, trying to get us off it. He is tricky, deceitful, cunning, and experienced. There are two sides to any pathway. If pride with guilt and shame are on the one side of humility, then what is on the other side? Perhaps the word "humble" might apply, correctly or incorrectly, but generally speaking, <u>false humility</u> is on the other side of the path or of the pendulum swing. The liar uses shame and guilt to lower our self-esteem and to make us feel unworthy. He would have us feel that we are not worthy of our unique gifts or, worse yet, that they don't exist. The deceiver would like to hide the truth from us or distort it in any way that he can. Humility is not about lowering our self-perception by allowing others to put us down or about lowering our self-esteem or our self-image, but about knowing our uniqueness through the eyes of the Lord. Acting as if we are less than our true selves would be false humility. Being a doormat is not virtuous! Satan would be happy to see us stuck in pride and/or false humility as long as he gets us off the narrow path. Humility is the courage of the heart necessary to defend against despair or intimidation. In humility, we can share our unique gifts with others to strengthen them but not to "lord over them." It can be summed up with this one-liner: "not thinking less of yourself, but thinking of yourself less."

We can overcome pride through <u>gratitude.</u> Gratitude as virtue is the offspring of humility. It is in true humility that we can see the beauty of our relationship with our loving God, and gratitude flows from that realization. We can choose to focus on God's creation and to see His work in all things. We can learn to give thanks and praise to God in exchange for our awesome gifts, which too often we take for granted. To react to a gift with pride is selfish in the sense that we think we have earned something and it is now ours to keep and to use however we so please. This isolates us from God, who has many more gifts that He would take pleasure in sharing with us. So too with false humility, when we are feeling down, we can elevate our spirits through gratitude.

> *You have been told O man, what is good,*
> *And what the Lord requires of you:*
> *Only to do the right and to love goodness,*
> *And to walk humbly with your God.* (Micah 7:8)

CHAPTER 11

From Envy to Brotherly Love

The story of Cain and Abel in Genesis 4 is a story of envy. Abel was a keeper of sheep, and Cain was a tiller of soil. They both brought an offering to the Lord. The Lord looked favorably on Abel's offering but not so with Cain's. Cain was stricken with envy to the point of murdering his brother. This story is almost unbelievable unless we recognize that we have a fallen nature that we have to face and, yes, that we need our Savior.

<u>Envy</u>, like lust or greed, can be characterized by an insatiable desire. Envy is similar to jealousy in that they are both feelings of dissatisfaction towards traits, status, abilities, or rewards. Jealousy by itself need not be a sin because it may be an awakening of a gift that needs to be developed. It can be a call from God. Envy goes one step further than jealousy in that the envious also desires the entity and covets it. It is a violation of two of the Ten Commandments, coveting of goods and desiring another person's spouse. This, of course, leads us away from our right relationship with God and is, therefore, a vice. It can lead to hatred of the other who has the coveted material, just as it was with Cain and Abel. It

begins with jealousy, and if not held in check, it can lead to anger, fighting, killing, or in severe cases, even war.

The virtue that is opposite to envy is <u>brotherly love</u> (kindness, admiration). It is exemplified by Elizabeth when Mary comes to visit. In Luke 1:41–42: *"When Elizabeth heard Mary's greeting, the baby leapt in her womb. Elizabeth was filled with the Holy Spirit and cried out in a loud voice: 'Blest are you among women and blest is the fruit of your womb'"* If only we could recognize that God chooses unique gifts for each of His creatures and so we will all be different! We need to appreciate the beauty and diversity of God's many gifts to His creation and to be grateful for the gifts of others. Positive affirmations and encouragement are fruits of this virtue. Just as humility is an appreciation of God's gifts to us personally, brotherly love is an appreciation of God's gift to others! They are both virtues that put us in right relationship with God.

It is the same in our relationships with neighbors. The virtuous person will attempt to see the God-given talent of a neighbor and positively affirm the gift, but also give credit to God. This is a most important virtue for administrators in choosing human resources, especially in Church circles, where we are trying to build the Body of Christ. If you have ever participated in a drama, you can appreciate the scenario. Each person has a gift or a part, but it is only fulfilled when all contribute. The performance comes together only with each member's input. Shakespeare once said that the whole world is a stage and we must each play our part. By contrast, there is nothing more pathetic than an envious person who cannot celebrate the blessings of a neighbor. It creates disharmony and disfigures the beautiful gift that God has given.

Incidentally, as parents, we have a loaded responsibility. We must observe and reflect on the God-given talents of our children. Then, in humility and generosity, we must enable and empower the growth and development of the talents of the child. Every child is unique and will have a different set of gifts that require empowering. If we are unclear as to the source of the gifts in others, the devil smiles. We become vulnerable to false virtue. Parents who don't see their children and grandchildren as gifts from God might want to see them as extensions of themselves. They forget that God is the author of all life. They want to take credit for the talent of their offspring. The same people start to brag about their children. They are inviting competition from other parents. "My child is better than yours." Children are the greatest vulnerability, and when one parent starts bragging, it makes it more difficult to see God's gift in right relationship. Bragging, an offspring of pride, is a very unflattering characteristic when encountered. In addition to denying the source of the gift, the parent jeopardizes the possibility for others to see and appreciate the gift or talent of the child. Bragging disfigures the gift, becomes a false virtue, distorts right relationship with God, and is alienating.

In searching for a false virtue to brotherly love, I have a question for you, my reader. Is the following an example of jealousy, stinginess, or simply self-centeredness? Or all three? Have you ever known someone who could not give positive affirmations when you were expecting them? Instead, they take your comments and remind you of a time when they accomplished the same task, except their accomplishment was bigger and better. They seem to be consumed with competition. How does that make you feel? It seems that there is nothing you can do that will make them acknowledge you. I have experienced this treatment from certain significant people in my life, people whom I would have expected to be happy for me. Instead, it seems to trigger an unhealthy insecurity that causes them to shut down, change the topic, or belittle my story, which I had been so very excited about. Once I begin to see this pattern in a relationship, I tend to withdraw, realizing that it stimulates their feeling of inadequacy and causes them to become defensive.

Whatever the name, it seems to fit the pendulum picture. In the middle, we have a God-given gift that is seen and appreciated by others (brotherly love). Some see the gift and want it for themselves and, in the extreme case, plot to claim the gift using any devious tactic they can come up with (envy). On the other side of the pendulum swing, is the person who refuses to see the gift and the inspired source of the gift and takes every step possible to discourage the development and use of the gift. Remember, the purpose of any spiritual gift is for the building up of the community.

To summarize, virtue is about having a right relationship with neighbors as well as God. It is about encouraging others in their virtue while discouraging them in their vice! So, we break the pattern of envy by true generosity (brotherly love) and also by prayer. Incidentally, the intention of the second joyful mystery, the Visitation, is for charity towards one's neighbor. Remember, charity is a disposition of the heart based on grace, whereas brotherly love is based on action, with love of God as their common source. Mary visited to share experiences, to offer encouragement and support, and to improve relationships, not only with her cousin Elizabeth but to develop a new one between the unborn Jesus and John the Baptist! Both women were completely in agreement and accepting of God's work, giving Him praise and thanksgiving. Thank God for the gift of our Blessed Mother!

CHAPTER 12

From Wrath to Patience

Father, forgive them, they do not know what they are doing.

(Luke:23:34)

Wrath is extreme anger, or uncontrollable rage, hatred, or a need for vengeance or revenge. People suffering from wrath will often resort to taking the law into their own hands if they feel that the justice system has failed them. They initiate conflict, hostility, and antagonism. In order to feed their need for wrath, they may turn to physical abuse, murder, or even genocide. Wrath is usually a need to do harm to others. It is contrary to the Commandments and isolates the person from God's love and mercy. Hence, it is one of the deadly sins. Dante, from The Divine Comedy once defined wrath as "love of justice perverted to revenge and spite."

The crucifixion of Jesus was clearly such an event. The Jews were waiting for a Messiah. They expected that the Messiah would be someone who would liberate them from the tyranny of the Romans. They expected a military leader who would use force.

By contrast, Jesus proclaimed the Kingdom of God, stating that it was already here. He performed miracles, and people flocked to be with him. All who touched him were healed. Many believed that he was the Messiah. Jesus provoked the establishment by challenging the laws that were considered to be most sacred. He healed on Sunday. He forgave sins. He called himself the Son of God. The authorities feared an uprising by his highly emotional moblike followers. The Jewish leaders were trying to trap Jesus with words. They were trying to find a contradiction in what He was saying, but they couldn't. As their frustration and anger grew, so did their resolve to crucify Him. Finally, with Judas's help, they found an opportunity. When Jesus was in the Garden of Gethsemane with the other apostles, the Roman soldiers, with the Jewish leaders, took Jesus. Being confused, Peter cut off the ear of a Roman soldier. After Jesus rebuked him and healed the ear back on, the apostles scattered.

The trial of Jesus became vicious. The many followers of Jesus turned on Him, not understanding the plan of the Messiah. Their zeal for His entry into Jerusalem on Palm Sunday was now replaced with anger and wrath, which was incited by the Jewish leaders. Even Pontius Pilate could not change their minds. They shouted to have Jesus crucified, and they became an uncontrollable mob.

The Jews, who had been victimized by the Romans, took the law into their own hands. They felt that justice was not serving them. They had a growing need to return the wrath of their frustration from their captivity. Jesus became the innocent victim and was crucified.

Patience is the virtue that offsets wrath. Patience is the belief that God is the author of justice. It is important to know that because it eliminates the need for revenge. Patience is an ability to know and wait for God to give direction.

Patience comes with prayer and dialogue with the Lord. We can let Him know our concerns, needs, and struggles. Through patience, we are moving closer to God, not away from Him as in wrath. He will respond in His way and His time. Remember, our perception of time is minuscule compared to His perception of eternity.

Jesus, unlike His followers, knew that He would be crucified. His mother, Mary, at a wedding feast in Cana, informed Him that they were out of wine. He replies: *"My hour has not yet come"* (John 2:4). His primary mission was to die for our sins and to be raised on the third day. The passion of our Lord was just that. His passion was an act of perfect love for us and nothing was going to stop him from having it fulfilled. During His passion, He became passive, patient, and totally focused. His hour was coming!

The patient person deals with others differently than the impatient. We react to others partly because we have an expected outcome. The impatient person wants the desired outcome immediately. If it's not on their schedule or is different in any way from their expectation, they might be irritated and react inappropriately. The patient person tries to understand the scenario without judgment and makes adjustments along the way until either the expectation is met or, perhaps, the expectation is modified. The patient one tries to see the good in others and encourages their growth.

My experiences with patience, or more correctly, impatience, are a result of being a parent, a classroom teacher, and simply a human being. One impatient reaction to a developing child, student, or vulnerable person can cancel much good work that has been done. Unkind words cannot be taken back. They either damage or fracture a relationship.

So, what could a false virtue look like? Like other false virtues, it looks like the virtue, but it is a movement away from God. Perhaps <u>apathy</u> looks like patience except there is no connection to God. As a matter of fact, apathy is a lack of caring.

Conflict is an inconvenient reality in life. <u>Aggressiveness</u> is an evil reaction to it and can be imagined as the extreme end of the pendulum swing. Many will deny aggression and react with more aggression when confronted. Or they might deny aggression by total removal from the conflict and the relationship that involves the conflict. Withdrawal is not necessarily virtuous, but it can be called <u>passive aggressive</u>. In conflict without resolution, there may be residues of guilt, anger, bitterness, and even revenge. Aggression and passive aggression are not evident in right relationship with one's neighbor and certainly not with God. <u>Assertiveness</u>, being in the middle of the aggression extremes, can be seen as a healthier, middle-of-the-way approach. Assertiveness in itself requires a lot of virtuous qualities such as patience, understanding, and sometimes forgiveness and mercy when the conflict has strayed from the middle ground into some form of aggression.

So, aggression-assertiveness-passive aggressive behavior might be more visible and usually the result of conflict with others, but it is a parallel to wrath-patience-apathy, which is more a result of internal conflict.

In praying the rosary and including the suggested intentions, we can easily conclude that among many other things, it is a prayer for virtue. The fourth decade of the sorrowful mysteries, Jesus carrying the cross, is for patient endurance. It is only in the perfect practice of the virtue of patience that we can ask for the forgiveness of those who have done us harm. Jesus on the cross is our perfect model.

CHAPTER 13

From Sloth to Diligence

> *The time for my dissolution is near. I have fought the good fight. I have finished the race. I have kept the faith. From now on a merited crown awaits me; on that Day the Lord, just judge that He is, will award it to me, and not only to me, but to all who have looked for His appearing with eager longing.*

> (2 Timothy 4:6–8)

Diligence is work or labor without distraction. It means "to keep on moving toward your goal without changing direction." One anonymous source says: "He who works diligently need never despair; for all things are accomplished by diligence and labor" while another says, "Patience and diligence, like faith, remove mountains." Being a virtue, and combined with humility, diligence means staying connected to God in your work. St. Paul wanted to stay focused on the final goal until the race was won.

Sloth is a vice that blocks diligence. It can include sadness, depression, or the inability to feel joy. Depression can lead to despair, suicide, and/or wrath. It can be triggered by a loss or lack of love. More importantly, sloth can be a name given to a lack of spiritual work. It can be a failure to use our God-given talents and treasures. Failing or refusing to develop spiritually is to become guilty of sloth. Sloth can be described as a sin of omission, whereby the guilty chooses to sit on the fence and do nothing. Ultimately, it is a rejection of God's love and grace. It is a rejection of His will. It is a rejection of His constant invitation for us to have a personal relationship with Him! It is a rejection of His constant desire to shower us with many beautiful gifts!

> *I know your deeds; I know you are neither hot nor cold. How I wish you were one or the other- hot or cold! But because you are lukewarm, neither hot nor cold, I will spew you out of my mouth!*

(Revelation 3:15)

I remember this Scripture passage being preached before Vatican II, when guilt and fear were popular in the homilies of the day. I was a child in the 1950s, but as a divorced man in the early 1980s, it was still etched on my soul. I did not want to be lukewarm, nor did I want to be vomited. Over the years, my faith has matured to the point where I now see God as merciful, forgiving, and always wanting to lavish gifts upon us to enable our growth. I still value the Scripture passage, but now I see it is an example of slothfulness, of someone unwilling to grow spiritually on the path to salvation. Are there people who assert that they have done more than their fair share and are unwilling to do more? Are there people who believe that they are already saved and don't have to do any more? Do some people attend only one of the celebrations during the Triduum instead of all three days and expect that their obligations have been met? Could this be the sin of sloth, or even presumption? There are many scenarios that could fit the example of lukewarm. My current pastor has preached that "the measure of love is to love without measure," and so we should never worry about being too hot!

What is the false virtue for sloth or diligence? Diligent work should not lead to burnout, but overindulgence can. Diligence is part of a healthy balance where all functions of a person's life are being dealt with. If the work becomes all-consuming, it means that Satan is getting us off the narrow path. Being overworked is an invitation to become assertive by asking for help, giving others a chance to help. This can lead to the building of the spiritual body. Going it alone can lead to passive aggressiveness and critical judgment of others. Being a workaholic is an addiction, and like any vice, it gets us further away from God. How many workaholics have ignored their families or other important relationships in the name of hard work? Instead of developing a right relationship with God, overindulgence can lead to idolatry where the work is worshiped instead of God. How many people fail to keep their Sunday worship a priority in favor of other activities that they rationalize to be more important? They have missed the mark because Satan was able to pull them away from God. Jesus invites all who are weary to come to Him, and He will give them rest: *"Come to me all you who are weary and find life burdensome and I will refresh you"* (Matthew 12:28).

CHAPTER 14

From Greed to Generosity

There are in the end three things that last: faith, hope and love and the greatest of these is love.

(1 Corinthians 13:13)

Love is a disposition of the heart, given by the grace of God, whereas generosity can be developed through habit formation.

<u>Generosity</u> is the virtue of giving unconditionally. It is an act of love based totally on free will without any expectation of a reward. It can be in the form of money, encouragement, hope, laughter, hospitality, or service. It is a decision to act in opposition to hate, contempt, envy, anger, and even indifference. There are times when the act of giving, although rooted in generosity, takes on a different name. Giving as a payment for a harm that was done is not generosity, but justice. Giving for the sake of reciprocity carries an expectation and is not generosity, but trade. Giving for the sake of loyalty can be a tradition or royalty, but not necessarily generosity. Free gifts are sometimes given as promotion, but

they carry an expectation. The appearance of generosity can be an act of manipulation. Remember, it is only when given with unconditional love that the name "generosity" can be perfectly applied.

<u>Greed</u> is the need for material possessions or wealth. A greedy person may resort to hoarding, theft, violence, robbery, or obtaining material possessions by way of trickery, violence, deception, or manipulation. Greedy people are easy to bribe and will take any bet or do anything for a dollar. The combination of greed, lust for power, and aggressiveness has been a deadly combination of vices in almost all the wars throughout history.

<u>Stinginess or miserliness</u> are only a part of greediness. Greed is a need for accumulation, whereas miserliness is an unwillingness to let go. "Even if I don't need it, nobody else is going to have it." It could be seen as false stewardship or false temperance and, therefore, false virtue. Miserliness is derived from the word "misery."

We see in Matthew 25 where the master calls in his three servants. The first receives five thousand talents and, with wise investing, doubles it. Similarly, the second receives two thousand talents and doubles them. The master is pleased with both. The third, however, buries his thousand talents, and when the master returns, he is angered. This servant did nothing, not even invest it in the bank. The master takes the money from him and gives it to the first servant, saying, *"Those who have will get more until they get rich, while those who have not will lose even the little they have. Throw this worthless servant into the darkness outside, where he can wait and grind his teeth"* (Matthew 25:29–30). Just as generosity is a decision to act in opposition to <u>indifference</u>, indifference can be a decision to oppose generosity and is, therefore, a false virtue.

It may seem overwhelming when we listen to the problems of the world. There are wars, famine, homelessness, and natural disasters, just to name a few. It can be depressing to see and hear about all the suffering in the world. Then, of course, there are the requests for help, all of which seem justifiable. There are so many that it is tempting to tune out. This temptation could be called indifference. We can argue that the money never gets to where it is needed; it either goes to administration or it is stolen before it reaches its required destination. This could be called rationalization or excuse making. What is required is stewardship. Education is the key to maximizing gift giving. For example, I support Peace and Development because their money is spent on community projects as opposed to going to an individual in a community. Generosity without indifference is the virtue. It requires faith that it will do some good.

How about the pattern of enabling? The term "enable" comes from 12-step language whereby the spouse of an alcoholic believes the promises of change that the addicted might make in order to create peace. The enabler may support lies, make excuses, and generally speaking, cover for the addicted. This support is given unknowingly with the primary motive of protecting the status quo or loyalty to the marriage. However, the enabler is missing the mark of generosity, which is to see and acknowledge the God-given goodness in the addicted. To enable is clearly false generosity. How about when parents support bad behavior? How about society as a whole? How much enabling is unknowingly going on? Enabling is the act of allowing a loved one to remain in false virtue, with the result of keeping the loved one away from God. It approaches indifference, although it may be far more emotional. Enablers know there is a problem; they just don't have a solution.

Satan is so tricky, and that is why we have a wonderful Savior. We must never forget to call on Jesus in times of temptation lest we fall. Thank you, Jesus, for being a merciful, forgiving, healing Savior who never abandons us even when we forget.

<u>Prayer of Serenity</u>
God, grant me the serenity to accept the things I cannot change, the courage to change the things I can, And the wisdom to know the difference.

Reinhold Niebur

CHAPTER 15

From Gluttony to Temperance

Gluttony can be the overindulgence of anything to the extreme, but especially food, drugs, alcohol, and sex. There are different ways of being caught up with gluttony. Any over involvement that becomes addictive can damage relationships. It can happen in sports, politics, work, and even church, where the addictive personality monopolizes the conversation and the eccentricity creates blindness to God's other gifts. The term workaholic is simply one result of over involvement when it is at the expense of other relationships. Wherever there is blindness, there is danger, and we need constant surveillance before we get too far into the vices that accompany them.

As Christians, we believe that we are temples of the Holy Spirit, and as such, we have a responsibility to live as healthily as we can. We must not sin against our bodies. Any excess of food, drugs, alcohol, and sex is an abuse of our temple of the Holy Spirit. A balanced diet with a balanced exercise program is a significant part of respecting our bodies. When lacking balance, we miss the goodness of the many benefits that are available in the variety of foods that God has given us so abundantly. We miss the beauty of all God's creation and especially His people when we interact with only other users who share the same addiction. It can apply to any activity where we become blinded to the beauty of a related activity. There is no limit to what we can enjoy as long as we don't become addicted to one and allow it to turn us into gluttons as a sad result.

As I mention in a future chapter, "The Slippery Slope," I am clearly opposed to abortion and euthanasia. Is it possible that partisan politics is sometimes an addiction when it is based on loyalty to the party while ignoring your right relationship with God? How can the Supreme Court overrule the Ten Commandments? What vices does Satan have working for such legislation?

Temperance is the virtue that opposes gluttony. Right relationship with God and neighbor is virtuous and must always be sought if we are to stay on the narrow path. Temperance means balance. Another term is stewardship. We are to utilize the gifts that He has given to us, especially time, money, and talent. These are to be used to thank and praise Him and to bring Him glory. Beware: any overuse can be gluttony, especially when other gifts are not being used or developed. A false virtue might be the result of an action being done for image or some harmful motive. Anorexia and bulimia are two obvious examples. They both oppose gluttony and are certainly not temperance. They are false virtues.

As a personal experience with gluttony, I can share the following story. In February 2002, I accepted a position to teach high school math in Canora, Saskatchewan, a small town of 2,500 people. I had moved from Calgary, where I had lived for 21 years. Real estate in small towns in Saskatchewan just had to be one of the world's best-kept secrets. In 2005, I started to realize that rentals could be a good supplement to retirement pension income, plus I had always had an interest in real estate. So, I was weighing an opportunity, and in 2006, I began a new career, that of a landlord and house owner.

My first purchase was a very solid investment. Possession date was July 1, 2006, and as a teacher, I had a two-month summer holiday. It was a front-back duplex with loads of potential for basement suites. I focused on the two main upstairs suites and had them ready for rental by September 1, 2006. The investment seemed very solid, and the banks had been generous. I kept focusing on the unfinished basements, both front and back, and started to develop two basement suites in the back of the property. It was a bi-level style with large basement windows. By May 1, 2007, they were completed and rented. It had been a learning experience with respect to codes, building permits, and old buildings. It was very satisfying, and I now owned a four-suite house.

During this period, there was a bit of a boom in the selling of real estate, and the market was brisk. I started to get an itch to have more. In the summer of 2007, I decided I would buy another property. Recognizing an opportunity, I purchased a two-bedroom bungalow for 18 thousand dollars—yes, 18 thousand! It even had a tenant in it. She was handicapped. Other than the low price, it was an opportunity because there were grants available for upgrading property with either seniors or handicapped people in them. I was preparing an application. It involved about 10 sub-trades, all requiring quotes. This was a challenge. People were busy, and the challenges of rewiring were big. I was told by one electrician that the best idea would be to demolish and build something bigger. He was probably right, but I wasn't prepared to go that big. My tenant didn't like the potential disruption in her life, so I dropped the idea. However, there was an energy-guide program available, so I tapped into that. Eventually, in 2011, after an unbelievable transformation, I sold the makeover for 97 thousand dollars. I had spent a large part of the difference between the purchase and selling price, but grants, rent, and some inflation had given me a healthy profit. I concluded two things based on my experience. The first is that there were, and still are, many opportunities for people to purchase property for less than 50 thousand dollars in Saskatchewan. Secondly, there is usually government grant money available for assistance in doing renovation work.

I probably should not have bought any more property, but in 2008, I continued. Here is where gluttony enters the picture! Lenders were encouraging. I had a teacher's salary, which looked very good on a mortgage application. Rents were increasing, and there were lots of renters. And I was on a roll. I was having fun. It was a novelty, and it was good for my ego. In a future application for a mortgage, one lender gave me not only the mortgage on the property that I was buying but enough to pay off a competitor's mortgage plus enough to have 10 thousand dollars left in my account for renovation purposes. I felt very lucky, motivated, and yes, even obsessive. So, I bought another house.

As a matter of fact, I continued buying, and by September 2009, I owned seven houses in total with 12 tenants. My expenses were being matched by my revenues. Rents were increasing, property values were increasing, interest rates were declining, and the government had decreased the educational portion of property taxes. Slowly, my debt load was decreasing as my assets were increasing. It all looked positive. I had retired from teaching in June 2009, and I was enjoying a new lifestyle and, indeed, a new retirement plan. However, nothing in life is ever guaranteed.

I will always remember the evening of June 30, 2010. From my home in Canora, I was watching the football rematch of the 2009 Grey Cup, in which the Saskatchewan

Roughriders lost to the Montreal Alouettes. The Riders had been penalized because of a 13th man on the field during an attempted field goal, enabling Montreal to re-kick a missed field goal, this time from five yards closer. It made the difference as they won the Grey Cup with a 16-point rally in the fourth quarter. The team and fans were devastated at the shocking turn of events! The replay game in 2010 had some parallel scenarios, but this time, the Riders won. Although it was very early in the season, it felt like redemption.

Along with many Rider fans, I was on an emotional high after the football victory UNTIL I discovered that during the football game, there had been a serious flood in Yorkton, where I had my revenue properties. It had destroyed my precious four-suite rental house! The force of the water had pushed in a concrete-block basement wall. Two other rental units had flooded with water levels as high as the window sills of the main floor, with the basements completely flooded. A fourth house had a water heater destroyed. I replaced the water heater within three days and kept my tenant. To summarize, my rentals had been decreased from 12 suites to five. I had gone from seven houses to four. My monthly revenue had decreased from seven thousand to three thousand dollars per month. My monthly expenses remained at seven thousand dollars per month. It was a life-changing event. The tenants were not injured, although they had witnessed the destruction of their rented homes. We were all in a state of shock and confusion. The first thing I had to do was return the July rent if it had been collected and to refund the damage deposits. My career as a landlord was ending just as quickly and as shockingly as the Roughriders had lost the Grey Cup game a year earlier with the 13th man on the field!

There are many chapters in my story of how I downsized after the flood, but they won't be included here. It was extremely stressful. From July 2010 to September 2014, I cleaned up my financial affairs that I had created and that had been caused by the flood. I had mortgages, lines of credit, credit cards, damage deposits, and maintenance items. I had claims through PDAP (Provincial Disaster Assistance Program) to process. I was walking a tightrope for six months, using all available credit that I had left. Being on a reduced rental income with my heavy debt load was not only stressful but very humbling! When help started coming from PDAP, they were fair. I renovated the four remaining houses and sold them. After four years of turbulence, I was finally free. As 2014 came to a close, I was free of debt, still having some assets and enough pension security to not have to worry about working. I was 66 years old and still very healthy, but with a lot less to do since my life as a landlord had ended.

I had time to reflect, and so, during the summer of 2014, I started to write a book. My book was going to be about vices and virtues. I started to reflect on my motives for buying real estate in the period up to June 2010. Had I been overtaken by pride? I was definitely proud of being a landlord, but there was a deeper sin. I had not prayed about my decisions. The first few had been well thought out, but each further purchase had become more compulsive. There was absolutely no doubt in my mind that I had been a glutton when it came to house buying: guilty not of overeating, but of overdosing on house buying. I had enjoyed it. It had felt like playing monopoly. Instead of living in balance, I had been consumed by the activities of buying, renting, and handling money. It is very ordinary to be the owner of a small business, which I was classified as, but was I doing God's will? I believe that God has a permissive will and a direct will. In his permissive will, He was allowing me to have some fun because He knows me and knows what I might do. The flood served as a lesson to not focus so much on money but to seek His will. He showed me His power in the flood, just as He had done to Noah. There is something very symbolic about water. Now I had my own personal experience!

Where was I going without God's intervention? Every coin has two sides, and admittedly, being a landlord had its dark side. I had to deal with selecting tenants, their irresponsible actions causing damage, and collecting rent. Some had lifestyles that were very problematic to me and to my neighbors. To see an emptied suite after the departure of a tenant was sometimes very shocking and disturbing. I began to discover that being a friend to tenants was a high risk. I experienced abuse based on my naivete in trusting people with their promises. Additional experiences included the discovery of a deceased tenant three days after her passing. Another tenant fell asleep while smoking and started a fire. Thanks to good neighbors who noticed the smoke, there was no damage. I discovered a skunk in a basement after a tenant moved out. They had left the basement window open as a parting gift. Before the flood, I was starting to question my own choices with certain tenants and my ability to do maintenance work and to realize that being a landlord was harder work than I had earlier anticipated. So, what seemed like a disaster could easily be argued as being a blessing in disguise.

With the benefit of hindsight, what was the lesson? God wants me to walk humbly with him and not to run ahead and make decisions on my own. Micah 7:8 states: *"You have been told, O man, what is good and what the Lord requires of you: Only to do the right and to love goodness, and to walk humbly with your God."* The virtues of humility, diligence, and temperance, when combined, give God glory. We are to know what our gifts and talents are and then, in diligence, serve by doing the work that He has designed for us to do!

I recently heard another Scripture passage that relates to my experience: Jesus explaining to His disciples the "Parable of the Seed." In Matthew 13:22, Jesus says, *"What was sown among briers is the man who hears the message, but the worldly anxiety and the lure of money choke it off. Such a one produces no yield."* Obviously, my experience as a landlord was not in line with the building of the Kingdom of God, but rather in line with the competitive world of greed. It was obvious that my choices did not yield any fruit.

Thank you, Lord, for the lessons that you are teaching me. Help me stay on the narrow path that leads to salvation!

CHAPTER 16

From Lust to Chastity

In 2 Samuel, we read about King David discovering Bathsheba while bathing. He lusted for her. He found out that she was the wife of Uriah the Hittite, who was away on a fighting campaign. David sent for her, had sex with her, and to his surprise, made her pregnant. When Uriah returned home, David encouraged him to sleep with Bathsheba so that it would be obvious to everyone that the child belonged to Uriah. Uriah did not go home. Instead, he spent the night with his fellow officers. David's plan had failed, so in order to keep the birth father a secret, he sent Uriah to the front lines, where inevitably he would be killed.

David now had three major sins to face. Lust was his first sin. He did not avoid the temptation, but because he was king and powerful, he knew that he could have her, and so he did. He became an adulterer but was caught by getting Bathsheba pregnant. Then, to continue the lie, he was instrumental in murder. Perhaps lusting was the least of his sins, but the results created a domino effect. Lusting, like any temptation, is not a sin if it is recognized and then resisted. If not, it becomes a whole legion of devils, which can include adultery, lies, and murder, with the result of causing mortal damage to the soul.

Lust is an insatiable need for sex or things of a sexual nature, including thoughts, desires, and actions. If this need is unfed, it can lead to masturbation, rape, and even bestiality. Lust is fed by the above means or even by viewing pornography. Sex was never meant to be a commodity for sale, nor for recreational purposes. Lusting and other vices have led to a very broken and distorted world.

God created man and woman in His image and likeness. The intention was for a homogenous lifelong relationship. Sexuality was a basis for loving and for procreation. Chastity is the virtue that offsets lust. It respects the beautiful gift of our sexuality. We must remember that we are temples of the Holy Spirit and, as such, we must keep our bodies pure. Chastity is a beautiful gift, and when practiced properly, it allows us to have a right relationship with God and our spouse. When chastity is honored, it is a mutual sexual act of consent between a male and female married couple. When sex is not mutually consensual, chastity is being violated. It is not meant to be selfish. Chastity is honored when both partners celebrate the beauty of making their partner happy. Chastity is about consideration for your partner's needs first, whereas lust is about your own selfish needs without any consideration for others.

As a young man, admittedly, I experienced lust for women. It was a factor in whom I would seek out. I did not have the social skills to evaluate who God might be directing to me. My value system and my social skills were both underdeveloped. I could add that they were two of the flat tires on my car that had my overinflated ego as its first tire. As an adult, I matured in my relationships with women, but at a high price of missed opportunity. In 1989, the Lord miraculously healed me of lusting in exchange for the virtue of chastity. With the benefit of hindsight, I can see it as a 180-degree conversion! Thank you, Lord!

An obvious false virtue towards chastity is when a body underbar{withdraws from one's partner} in order to manipulate him or her. It may be connected to revenge, a disagreement, or any number of unresolved issues. Differences should lead to discussion, understanding, and acceptance if/when they still exist. Healthy discussion should lead to intimacy. Remember, virtue, including chastity, is a right relationship between God and the couple. That is why it is said that Christ is the center of any successful Christian marriage. There is fewer than one divorce in a thousand marriages when married Catholic couples worship on Sunday together and pray together daily.

As a man, I have come a long way in appreciating the beauty of women. More and more, I love women not as objects, but as beautiful creatures of God. Women have played a major role in my spiritual journey. When I began it in 1989, hugging became an obvious difference in my cultural practices. The feeling of acceptance and peace far outweighed any feelings of lust that I had ever experienced before. I had been so broken. I needed hugging so desperately that I accepted hugs even from men. Admittedly, I found it strange at first, but it is now a part of who I am when in Christian circles. I know that it is not only healing but also a way to share in the love and joy of the Lord. Prudishness is perhaps a false virtue in the sense that it discourages the flow of what is acceptable and possible. A prudish person might not be able to enjoy the well-intended affections of others.

So, to summarize, chastity is a right relationship with God and with our brothers and sisters. There is no room for lust, lewdness, nor prudishness, nor any reaction that distracts our focus from God. It is total purity. Incidentally, when we pray the rosary, the intention of the second sorrowful mystery, the Scourging at the Pillar, is for chastity.

CHAPTER 17

Others

Vices and virtues in isolation can be simply defined. When the seven deadly sins are compared with the seven capital virtues, the pendulum swing seems to be a good metaphor. The reality is that life is far more complicated than a pendulum swing, but would it be correct to say that many of life's complicated events still fit into the metaphor?

One such complex topic is that of human rights versus the authority of leaders. It has been central to the history of political development since the beginning of time, and it still exists today. In the first three hundred years of Christianity, the Romans ruled mercilessly, and martyrdom was very common. Since the time of Constantine (300s AD), the Church and the king worked together to control the minds and to maintain the loyalty of the people. The king would provide protection in exchange for taxes and even indulgences. Perhaps for the majority, security and stability were the rewards of this arrangement. The political situation through the ages had many challenges, but in order to keep the discussion simple, the "divine right of kings" was a popular theme that survived for centuries. The rights of individuals were subordinated to the rule of the king with the support of the Church. One event that began to change this balance was when Martin Luther challenged the Pope's authority in 1518, triggering the Protestant Reformation. The authority of kingdoms and the Church continued to erode until the French Revolution. Democracy in France was replacing the monarchy and the influence of the Church. During the American Revolution, the authority of the Church was separated from the control of the state so that no one religion could dominate. Institutions were compromising in order to respect the rights of all its religions. No specific religion was being respected as the sole authority because it might conflict with the rights of another religion. Remember a time when Sunday shopping was not allowed? It began as a compromise respecting the fact that the Jewish Sabbath was a Saturday.

The 1960s represent an explosion of freedom of expression and rebellion against institutions. Many apparently positive changes were taking place with regard to civil rights. Remember when, in 1936, Hitler condemned Jesse Owens, an African-American track star who won four gold medals in the Berlin Olympics? Soon after, African-Americans started to take their rightful place in the world by entering into other sports, entertainment, and even politics. President Obama became the first president of the USA with an African-American background.

And now we have President Trump, who has given support to white supremacists and is engaged a war against journalism and all forms of media coverage. Everything seems to be fake news. How much hatred was thrown around in the name of free speech during the presidential election of 2016? There doesn't seem to be any boundaries between freedom of speech and hatred in speech.

We seem to be living in a moral vacuum. After all, relativism teaches that all sets of morals are to be accepted and that no set of morals is to dominate any other set. It seems that we have taken away the authority of the Church from society and have replaced it with self-centered individuals who are making demands without any regards to the moral principles of others. How else could abortion, and now euthanasia, be justified when one set of morals, as outlined in the Ten Commandments, forbids killing?

Furthermore, taxpayers are expected to pay for this acceptance of relativism, which now demands that all moral standards have equal acceptance and equal rights in accordance with the Universal Declaration of Human Rights of the United Nations, which, in some extreme cases, actually overrules Church teachings. In Canada, we recently paid over ten million dollars in compensation to a child-soldier-killer named Khadr because, as a prisoner, he had been mistreated. We have recently spent over three million dollars to settle with Duffy, who challenged the legality of certain expenses while acting as a sitting senator. Incidentally, both cases have further unresolved issues that will cost taxpayers even more. Khadr is insisting on visiting rights with his sister, who is a declared supporter of the Taliban in Pakistan. How much money is being spent on litigation to prove who is right? Although this may sound like an exaggeration, there is truth to it. Without a set of clear moral standards, issues are sorted out in the courts. Have we seen the worst of it? Or are institutions continuing to lose control of society? This is the price we pay for living in a moral vacuum. I would like to think that the pendulum has swung from limited human rights under oppressive regimes to regimes where human rights are causing a heavy burden on governments to the point where society is being oppressed.

So, where is the virtue or the center of the pendulum swing? The extreme cases are both vices. I would suggest that when the Church had influence, it was in the center of the pendulum swing in the position of virtue. Many would disagree, of course, but perhaps the method of rule of the Church was the problem, not the actual teachings of the Church. The baby was thrown out with the bathwater! It has been removed, and now I would suggest that it has been replaced by nothing but a moral vacuum. How else can you explain abortion and euthanasia? Politicians would argue that it is in the Universal Declaration of Human Rights. However, this declaration does seem to replace the authority of God, which makes it idolatry. It is now acceptable for a political leader to say that in order to run in an election, you must be "pro-choice," implying that "pro-life" is unacceptable.

To summarize, society has eliminated Church authority, but at what price? I would argue that this is an example of a large pendulum swing from one extreme to another. At one end of the pendulum swing, the freedoms of individuals were stifled and the free choice that God gave us was controlled. Now, with freedom of speech embracing hatred, we seem to have lost everything that is good. Using the Canadian federal election as an example, honest politicians who project balanced budgets are defeated by cunning politicians who buy voters like prostitutes. The highest bidder wins the election. They started the 2015 campaign by stating that all their candidates must be pro-choice. By the way, this seems to be a contradiction because, once an abortion is committed, there is no longer any choice for the mother or innocent baby whose life has just been terminated. How about this as a conspiracy theory? Acceptance of being a pro-choice candidate serves as part of a screening test. It can be readily assumed that the same candidate will support euthanasia and legalizing marijuana. Once the candidate passes the test, obedience in accepting all other immoral issues that the government might propose can be assured. This might seem to be a little bit of ranting, as it is only a small factor in the total picture, but it does show how a political party can make Church authority and its teachings seem irrelevant in a political world. After all, the best way of separating Church from state is to completely shut the Church out. John F. Kennedy once stated, "The further that the truth is removed, the more it is hated."

The pendulum swing begins with absolute authority and absolute rule and swings to anarchy, but where are the virtues in this political dilemma? My purpose is not to discuss politics and to discredit leaders, but to demonstrate how the pendulum example in my previous chapters applies to real life, with politics as an example. The real challenge in any situation is to find the center of the swing, that is, the position of virtue. The problem with partisan politics is that the opposition is always reminding the party in power of the wrongs that they have committed. The devil is being worshiped when talent and money are wasted on studying how the crime was committed and who is guilty. If political institutions were virtuous, they would be looking at the good that they could be doing for their citizens instead of wasting money on litigation, war, and extravagant lifestyles for the few.

I remember a priest friend of mine, 25 years ago, being asked to give a talk on the New Age movement. He began his presentation with a parallel to counterfeit bills. Would the first step be to study as many counterfeit bills as possible, noting their differences? Or, by contrast, would it be better to have a standard to compare to? He asserted that you need to study the real bill and get to know every detail about it. Then, when you encounter the phony, you will be able to see that it is different from the authentic. And so it is with the New Age movement. Get to know the authentic person of Jesus Christ through the Gospels, Church teachings, or any other related resources that focus on Christ. Get to know

Church history and the heresies that were debated years ago. Most controversial topics are simply a recycling of old heresies that seemed logical at the time but that through Church discernment were proven to be false. For example, Arianism was a big one, and I have read arguments on how this false belief has been preserved and has shown itself in modern times. It is sufficient to conclude that we need to cling to the authentic in order to avoid the phony. This conclusion is true whether the topic is counterfeit money, the New Age movement, politics, or a discussion on vices. The reality is that Satan loves confusion and chaos. He will do anything to have us believe that the counterfeit is real. He would like us to believe that there are alternate facts, alternate truths, and false truths (clearly a contradiction). So, the lesson is that we need to learn about Jesus, for He alone is "the way, the truth, and the life" (John 14:6). This is how we must fill our moral vacuum. There is an overabundance of vices in the world, but we do not need to study them. We need simply to recognize that they are an attempt by Satan to destroy our right relationship with God, which can be "simply beautiful and beautifully simple." As in the Garden of Eden, it is the devil who is always tempting us to desire more than we need.

When I was doing the Spiritual Exercises of St. Ignatius in the early 1990s, I encountered the word "detachment," meaning a freedom of desire from anything worldly. Jesus was displaying detachment during the temptations in the desert. The devil tempted Him, and Jesus remained focused on the Word of God.

Mark also emphasizes detachment in this Scripture passage:

> *And as he was setting out on his journey, a man*
> *ran up and knelt before him, and asked him, "Good*

Teacher what must I do to inherit eternal life?" And Jesus said to him, "Why do you call me good? No one is good but God alone. You know the commandments: Do not kill. Do not commit adultery. Do not steal. Do not bear false witness. Do not defraud. Honour your father and mother." And he said to him, "Teacher, all these things I have observed from my youth." And Jesus looking upon him, loved him, and said to him, "You lack one thing; go, sell all you have, and give to the poor, and you will have treasure in heaven; and come follow me." At that saying his countenance fell, and he went away sorrowful; for he had great possessions.

(3:17–22)

One lesson in the above reading is that the riches of the world can be a barrier to becoming a follower of Jesus Christ. As in the example of the counterfeit money, detachment is the freedom to ignore anything phony, which the riches of the world are if they are an obstacle to seeking Jesus. Seek only what is real. It is a tremendous spiritual gift, or virtue, in the sense that temptations are so much easier to resist when we understand detachment. Temptation gives us a chance to practice it. The next time the Devil tempts you, say, "Thank you, Satan. I need the practice to avoid you," and then add, "Praise you, Jesus. I love you." Finished! Satan and his temptation flee at the precious name of Jesus.

One of the vices or sins that requires further emphases is that of idolatry. People who miss Mass on Sunday are not displaying detachment. They are placing some object or situation ahead of their right relationship with God. Any influence from any vice is the result of a lack of detachment. When the first commandment, "Thou shalt not have false gods before me," is violated, idolatry is committed. It is due to being attached to worldly enticements, which is contrary to the virtue of detachment. I remember someone saying that the most important commandment is the first one because, when we have another god, all the other commandments lose their significance.

> *Take, Lord, and receive all my liberty,*
> *my memory, my understanding, and my entire will,*
> *all that I have and possess,*
> *You gave it all to me; to you I return it.*
> *All is yours; dispose of it entirely according to your will.*
> *Give me only the grace to love you*
> *for that is enough for me.*

> (*Spiritual Exercises* 43, 231–35)

PART FOUR

THE NARROW PATH TO HOLINESS

You, too, must set apart, then, the clean animals from the unclean and the clean birds from the unclean, so that you may not be contaminated with the uncleanness of any beast or bird or of any swarming creature in the land that I have set apart for you. To me, therefore you shall be sacred; for I, the Lord, am sacred, I, who have set you apart from the other nations to be my own.

(Leviticus 20:25–26)

Against the World

Have no love for the world,
nor the things that the world affords.
If anyone loves the world,
the Father's love has no place in him,
for nothing that the world affords
comes from the Father.
Carnal allurements, enticements for eye,
the life of empty show---all these are from the world.
And the world with its seductions is passing away
But the man who does God's will endures forever.

(1 John 2: 15–17)

CHAPTER 18

The Narrow Path

Enter through the narrow gate. The gate that leads to damnation is wide, the road is clear, and many choose to travel it. But how narrow is the gate that leads to life, how rough the road, and how few there are who find it!

(Matthew 7:13–14)

"I am indeed going to prepare a place for you and then I shall come back and take you with me, that where I am you also may be. You know the way that leads to where I go." "Lord," said Thomas, "we do not know where you are going. How can we know the way?" Jesus told him: "I am the way, and the truth, and the life; no one comes to the Father except through me. If you really knew me, you would know my Father also. From this point on you have known him; you have seen him."

(John 14:3–7)

Truly, I assure you: whoever does not enter the sheepfold through the gate but climbs in some other way is a thief and a marauder.

(John 10:1)

Jesus is being described as the way. Whether it is called the path, the way, or the gate, it is referring to the road that leads to Heaven. It is a narrow path! The distractions are many! How can we stay on the straight and narrow path? It is only by the grace of God and our own disciplined effort. The two must be inseparable. Obviously, the grace of God is necessary for us to do our part, and yet our constant diligence while growing in virtue is equally necessary.

Can you picture yourself on a trail in the woods, perhaps in the mountains? You probably prepared for this hike. Your level of fitness, diet, familiarity with the trail, maps, and choice of companions were perhaps part of your preparation. You may have talked to others about their experience and were motivated by them. There are signposts along the trail to keep you going towards your destination, just as there are on the straight and narrow path that leads to Heaven. Our narrow path, too, has many signposts, but for us, our goal is Heaven. So, what are our signposts? They could be the virtues. Stay on the path of faith, hope and charity, humility, brotherly love, diligence, patience, temperance, chastity, generosity, and other virtues that have been discussed, and even some that have not been discussed.

Along the way, there are many distractions. Remember the four voices mentioned in chapter eight? It is obvious that the voice of the Holy Spirit wants to keep us on the narrow path. I fear, however, the voices of Satan through peer pressure and patterns. Are there signposts for these other voices? There are, but we have to watch our map closely. In other words, we need to meditate and reflect daily on our activities.

Suppose that one sign invited you to become a great hockey player, with years of excellent pay, benefits, glory, and all the pleasures that go with a privileged lifestyle. Would you be distracted off the path? Is it a sin to want wealth? Just think of all the good you could do in the building of the Kingdom of God with wealth. However, once you are in the group of players, you realize that Sunday Mass is an inconvenience or, worse yet, that there is no longer any time for it. There are further distractions. None of your peers choose Mass over hockey. Why should you? Some of your peers have beautiful girlfriends or, even worse, many girlfriends, and these guys own the nicest cars. Could you have this also? Are peer pressure and vices now pulling you away from God? You are being drawn into the modern world dominated by secularism and relativism. It is a world that is increasingly rejecting God's laws, teachings, and the Church. Your relationship with God is now being challenged, compromised, and is deteriorating. Hockey is just one example, and there are so many more.

Wikipedia defines secularism as "the principle of the separation of government institutions and persons mandated to represent the state from religious institutions and religious dignitaries." The evolution of secularism can be found in history. For centuries, kingdoms and the Church were in an alliance on the caring of the citizens. The French Revolution, which rejected the alliance, is a milestone in the development of secularism. Governments have been rejecting Church law ever since. Changes have resulted, and we are approaching a world where every single opinion has equal value no matter what the basis of it is.

In our Western world, we now have Sunday shopping. Christmas, Easter, and All Saints Day (Halloween) have been secularized to the point where some people are offended if the word "Christ" is found in the word "Christmas." It is gaining popularity to say, "Happy Holidays," instead of "Merry Christmas." The symbol in the secular world for Easter is the Easter Bunny, while the Triduum is participated fully by few. Few Catholics celebrate both All Saints Day and All Souls Day. Instead, the highlight is to mask their children and take them trick or treating.

It suffices to say that secularism, with its separation of church and state, and relativism have joined forces to combat Church teachings through peer pressure and political manipulation. They are tools that Satan is using quite successfully in getting pilgrims off the path. Political systems such as capitalism and communism are enemies of getting us off the straight and narrow path. Capitalism encourages pride, greed, envy, gluttony, and licentiousness (the attitude that privilege for a select few is a God-given right). Communism stifles creativity, freedom, and excellence. History teaches that the Church has suffered much under Communist regimes. Secularism dictates the rights of individuals at the expense of moral dignity.

Relativism is a theory that conceptions of truth and moral values are not absolute, but are relative to the persons or groups holding them. In other words, truth, values, and criteria for judgment may vary from one culture or environment to another. It is this approach that entitles everyone to have their own opinion. As society tries to become more tolerant and accepting of each other, universal standards may be weakened or compromised.

At first, the theory might seem like a peaceful solution in a very troubled world. When two or more conflicting viewpoints are co-existing, compromise sometimes will work. Daylight savings time for summer and standard time for winter seems to be working as a compromise. In Saskatchewan, where the time zone splits the province, we do not compromise, and we have only standard time. For those who like to argue, there are two viewpoints. We live in the Central Standard Time Zone or, as legislated when the debate was settled in the provincial chambers once and for all, in the Mountain Daylight Savings Time Zone.

When free-trade agreements are drawn up or when unions and associations are being negotiated, it seems that a position of minimal loss or maximum gain is sought for both parties. It is easier to compromise if one can see that the other side is negotiating in good faith.

Unlike some differences that can be settled without either side taking a total loss, the concept of relativism seems to be an exception. If all religions were to discuss the concept of accepting the fifth commandment of God or rejecting it, they would almost certainly agree that "thou shalt not commit murder." They would also probably agree that abortion and euthanasia are a violation of the fifth commandment because they are both acts of terminating life.

So, why can't they agree? They have been subjected to the principle of secularism. The state and religion are to be separated, meaning that the Ten Commandments, a basis of Judeo-Christian faith, have no place in government. As a matter of fact, politicians who want to succeed in Canada feel obligated to put party consensus ahead of their own personal faith beliefs. How else can a political party justify that in order to be a candidate, you must be pro-choice? Does that mean that pro-life is no longer considered to be a valid choice?

In 1963, Cardinal Ratzinger stirred the pot by arguing against relativism with a nine-hundred-page theological document. It was entitled *Dominus Jesus*. It stated that "Jesus is Lord and as Catholics we must live our lives as if

Jesus is Lord." It reinforced Catholic teaching that despite worldly developments, we as Catholics are not to accept nor to participate in activities without first honoring our own beliefs. For example, we are to accept the fact that "Jesus Christ is our Lord and Savior." It is our absolute truth, and we must reject what relativism is trying to get us to say: "In my opinion, Jesus is Lord, but you are entitled to your opinion." If morals are diminished by the belief that everyone's morals have equal value, then why are we so surprised that we have terrorism being spread by jihadists throughout the world? After all, are the followers of relativism not promoting the concept that all values are valid? Why would jihadists be exempt from relativistic theory? Relativism is on a slippery slope without boundaries.

> *"You are the Messiah," Simon Peter answered, "the Son of the living God!" Jesus replied, "Blest are you, Simon son of John! No mere man has revealed this to you, but my Heavenly father. I for my part declare to you, you are 'Rock' and on this rock I will build my church, and the jaws of death shall not prevail against it. I will entrust to you the keys to the kingdom of heaven. Whatever you declare bound on earth shall be bound in heaven; whatever you declare loosed on earth, shall be loosed in heaven."* (Matthew 16:16–20)

So, who is on the path? I believe that the Catholic Church is the leader of pilgrims on the path. I believe that the Holy Spirit of God has guided the Church through two thousand years of societal upheavals. We have a lineage of popes back to St. Peter. We have a history of teaching found in the Magisterium and the Catholic Catechism. We have a history of saints and a bloodline of martyrs. After all, how many institutions, powers, or nations have survived for two thousand years? How many institutions, powers, or nations have a promise by Jesus Christ that the jaws of death will not prevail against them?

So, who else is on the path? Anyone can get on the path, but it is by the grace of God through Baptism that we need to enter. We then become children of God, and he guides us. What happens to those who don't find the path or believe that there is no journey or fail to get back on it? Can you dare to take a chance? I can't.

James makes the narrow path very black and white. James 4:4 states, *"O you unfaithful ones, are you not aware that love of the world is enmity to God? A man is marked out as God's enemy if he chooses to be the world's friend."* If this sounds too difficult, James has the solution. James 4:7–10 goes on to say, *"Therefore submit to God; resist the devil and he will take flight. Draw close to God and he will draw close to you. Cleanse your hands, you sinners purify your hearts, you backsliders. Begin to lament, to mourn and to weep; let your laughter be turned into mourning and your joy into sorrow. Be humbled in the sight of the Lord and he will raise you on high."*

The path is long, so how do we know that we are on it? The gifts and fruits of the Spirit provide us with consolation. Paragraphs #1831 and #1832 of the Catholic Catechism are worth quoting: "The seven gifts of the Holy Spirit are wisdom, understanding, counsel, fortitude, knowledge, piety, and fear of the Lord. They belong in their fullness to Christ. They complete and perfect the virtues of those who receive them. They make the faithful docile in readily obeying divine inspirations."

The fruits of the Spirit are perfections that the Holy Spirit forms in us as the first fruits of eternal glory. The tradition of the Church lists twelve of them: charity, joy, peace, patience, kindness, goodness, generosity, gentleness, faithfulness, modesty, self-control, and chastity. Have you ever experienced joy or peace without any explanation, as if it is bubbling over from within? Is that an experience of the divine fruit of the Spirit? The path is long and narrow, but the fruits of the Spirit keep us nourished, encouraged, and diligent. We simply need to recognize that the Holy Spirit is present and leading us on to our final goal! The path is not easy, so we need to be aware of the slippery slope and the path to holiness, which are the subjects of the next two chapters.

CHAPTER 19

The Slippery Slope

Staying on the narrow path requires 24/7 watchfulness. It requires many forms of guidelines. We have guardian angels, a communion of saints, Church teachings, sacraments, and the Holy Spirit, which contribute to an informed conscience. We have ways of getting back on the path when we fall off. We have a God of mercy and forgiveness and the gift of salvation through Jesus Christ our Lord and Savior. He has instituted the Church and the sacraments, especially that of Reconciliation, for when we fall. It is not an easy task, but it is our part of our mission. Remember, "we have been created to know God, to love God and to serve God so that we may one day be happy with Him in Heaven" (Baltimore Catechism). So how does Satan get us off the path?

There is the example of boiling a frog. If you put a frog into boiling water, it will jump out. But if you put a frog into water at room temperature, it will stay. Then you slowly add boiling water to the mix and then finally turn up the heat until the water is boiling. The poor frog has been slowly adjusting to a deathly situation until it is too late.

I remember hearing a country and western song about a recovering alcoholic saying that the first drink is one too many and a thousand aren't enough. Like the frog or the drinker, we can be lulled into thinking that we can turn back after Satan gives us a taste of his poisonous pleasure.

We must remember the Ten Commandments. The first commandment says: "I am the Lord thy God and thou shall not have strange gods before me." It is like a first drink for an alcoholic or a pot of lukewarm water for a frog. All the other commandments are in danger after the first one is broken. The Ten Commandments were given to the Israelites during a time when there were many strange gods in a very pagan world. Pagans were worshiping heavenly bodies, animals, weather events, or precious jewels made for themselves. The Jews worshiped the one true God, who made all these things. The Old Testament has several accounts where the one true God of the Jews proved to be more powerful than any of the other false gods. Our world is filled with idolatry or the worship of false gods. Relativism, secularism, and their offspring – the Universal Declaration of Human Rights – are tools of the slippery slope and have enabled abortion and euthanasia to become rooted in our modern-day society.

In February 2015, the Supreme Court of Canada ruled in favor of assisted suicide. The government of Canada was given one year to legislate how euthanasia is to be implemented. Taking one's own life is now a right, and Parliament is to decide on the rules. This was legislated without any discussion in Parliament and has been accepted as the law of the land.

Abortion and euthanasia are both forms of killing. They are both violations of the Ten Commandments. The fifth commandment simply states: "Thou shalt not kill." How did we get forced into a situation where the laws of God are going to be violated in the name of compassion? Canada is a country based on Judaic Christian values, but because of the acceptance of relativism, everyone's morals have the same right to co-exist. It has led to the Universal Declaration of

Human Rights, which is based on pragmatism, secularism, and individual rights at the expense of communal rights and, yes, even at the expense of following the Ten Commandments. Remember, the commandments are not advice for healthy living, nor are they simply choices. They are commandments (rules and obligations)! It is a case of freedom gone mad and out of control! Freedom is NOT the right to do what you want, but the right to do what you ought!

We used to accept God as the author of life and death, didn't we? Since 1974, there have been over three million abortions in Canada! Which gets more attention from the news media, abortion or terrorism? Whose rights are being ignored: the rich and the powerful or the weakest members of society? The unborn have no rights and no voice and are clearly being ignored. The abortion issue has been volatile, divisive, and even violent since it was legally accepted.

We have clearly rejected God as the author of life and death. This now raises many questions. If not God, <u>who will be the author</u>? Who will have the right to make the decision? Who will play God? Will there be a line-up for the job, or will it be someone who is forced to kill despite their own moral convictions? Once it becomes legalized, the social stigma against suicide will be eliminated, and consciences will be conditioned so that the masses of people will now celebrate suicide, just as discussions on abortion have been muted.

<u>Who will be the recipient</u> of euthanasia? There have been some very strong cases made from actual examples. The Sue Rodriguez and Robert Latimer cases have pulled at the heartstrings of Canadians, with growing popularity for legalizing the movement. The government of Canada is now going to spend far too many resources on the question. The issue of euthanasia is now on the <u>slippery slope</u>, and the Devil is laughing. Resources will be spent on discussions, legalizing,

and litigation instead of palliative care. Lines in the sand will be difficult to draw because there is always another case that is almost as justifiable as the last one. There will be a domino effect on leniency, and people will choose suicide instead of offering their suffering towards salvation.

The next issue will be that of <u>who pays for it?</u> How much has been spent to date? There was already much lobbying and litigation long before the recent expense for the time of the nine judges of the Supreme Court of Canada, who declared that assisted suicide is a right. Would it not be simpler to say that God is the author of life and death and let Him decide when life on earth ends? The next question is that of universality and who pays the bill. Will it end up like abortion, with the taxpayers paying for something that is contrary to their morals? We will end up paying for the choices of others that contradict our own personal values. We are paying to have our own values eroded when we pay for euthanasia instead of palliative care. Can this still be called democracy?

Beware of the slippery slope, for once on it, our ability to stop a crash is handed over to others to control. The New Age movement has been an enticement used by Satan very successfully in recent years. It is based on the false supposition that we have the power to satisfy ourselves. It rejects the belief that we are created with a longing in our souls that only God can fill. The New Age movement teaches us how to fill it for ourselves. The power of the Holy Spirit is denied and is replaced by the belief that we can become our own god. Our Catholic Church is being drained by false teachings, and we continue to allow others to stumble, hoping that they will find their way. O, how we need a Savior!

I told the story before about my priest friend who was asked to give a talk on the New Age movement because it was recognized as a "cancer" to the Church. He compared it to counterfeit money and advised that we study the real thing before getting to know all the counterfeits. So it is with the New Age movement. Compared to Christianity, it is counterfeit in its many forms. So, why spend any time in acknowledging its phoniness when we can study the beauty of Christianity, increasing our appreciation for its authenticity. We need to pray for and practice prudence. Satan is so successful because he knows Scripture, and he knows how to twist it in order to create deception. In John 10:10–12, Jesus says:

> *The thief comes only to steal and slaughter and destroy. I came that they might have life and have it to the full. I am the good shepherd; the good shepherd lays down his life for the sheep. The hired hand, who is no shepherd nor owner of the sheep, catches sight of the wolf coming and runs away, leaving the sheep to be snatched and scattered by the wolf.*

When "*have it to the full*" is taken out of context, the door is open for New Age thinkers to pursue anything that they desire because God willed it. It is an invitation for licentiousness. The reality is that the way of the cross is denied by the "hired hand." I was at a New Age celebration before my honeymoon experience. Even at that time, the deception was obvious. There was no acknowledgment of Jesus nor the power of the Holy Spirit. It was focused totally on "I," which, coincidentally, is the middle letter in both "sin" and "pride." I was distraught at how the audience was sucking up the deceptions. I thank God for my gifts, which enabled me to discern the lies.

It seems that the glamor of evil has many successes because we forget the words of Jesus in John 14:6: *"I am the way, and the truth, and the life; No one comes to the Father, but through me."* He didn't say He was one of many ways. He said that He is THE ONLY WAY. So, why do we spend so much time, energy, and money on false prophets when we can spend our time on the path that Jesus is constantly inviting us to travel on with Him and our beloved brothers and sisters who are also accepting his invitation. There is no other choice! He wants us on the path that leads to holiness.

CHAPTER 20

The Path to Holiness

Finally, draw your strength from the Lord and his mighty power. Put on the armor of God so that you may be able to stand firm against the tactics of the devil. Our battle is not against human forces, but against the principalities and powers, the rulers of the world of darkness, the evil spirits in regions above. You must put on the armor of God if you are to resist on the evil day; do all that your duty requires, and hold your ground. Stand fast, with the truth as the belt around your waist, justice as your breastplate, and zeal to propagate the gospel of peace as your foot gear. In all circumstances hold faith up before you as your shield; it will help you extinguish the fiery darts of the evil one. Take the helmet of salvation and the sword of the Spirit, the word of God.

(Ephesians 6: 10–17)

The work of staying on the path is challenging. Can it be done without the Grace of God? Not a chance! Can we stay on the path by grace only? This question has led to much discussion throughout Church history. The Catholic Church teaches that salvation comes from grace and good works. Throughout the history of Christianity, there have been many different perceptions of good works and how they must be included in working out our salvation.

Paul argued that salvation comes from faith in Jesus Christ. He was arguing with the teachings of Judaism, which focused on the letter of the Judaic laws. When he said that salvation comes from faith alone, he was referring to good works as following the letter of the law, which he stated was not necessary for salvation. He was not referring to good works in the same way that James did.

James continued the discussion, saying that faith without good works is dead. Faith alone, without works, could be sloth or presumption. Idleness and especially not doing spiritual work is sloth. How can a believer sit back and do nothing in response to the tremendous gifts that Christ has bestowed on us? Is it possible? Not a chance! The Bible cannot be taken in isolated parts, as shown by Paul and James. We cannot pick and choose the parts that we like and discard the rest. It has taken the Church two thousand years under the guidance of the Holy Spirit to develop its teachings, which say that salvation comes from faith and good works. If good works were excluded, why would Matthew 25 be part of the Bible?

The path to holiness is also very challenging. We need to be aware of the narrow path, to seek grace for discernment on the journey and the ability to reflect on holiness. This is another form of good work, that of transforming our souls to perfect holiness.

I was blessed by the image of holiness below. It begins with the cross. There are three relationships in my picture. The first is the vertical element of the cross. It represents <u>my relationship with Jesus,</u> who died on the cross for me. He is calling you and me to holiness through the power of the cross.

He reminds us and commands us to love one another, and hence, the second relationship, <u>our relationship with one another,</u> is symbolized by the horizontal arm of the cross. Our faith is not in isolation from others, and it cannot be practiced without the Church. We need both the love of Christ and brotherly love. Also, we need it to flow in both directions. Love, like blood, has to flow in order to be healthy and fruitful.

illustration by
sara kreutzer

In Mark 12:31, Jesus commands us to love our neighbors as ourselves. So, the third set of relationships is <u>with ourselves</u>. We need to be healthy and whole to be holy. Are wholly and holy synonyms? In the picture, there are four quadrants that circle the intersection of the vertical and horizontal. In my picture, they represent body, intellect, emotions, and the will. The four parts must be in harmony in order to best serve God. We are taught that we must love God with our whole <u>mind</u> (intellect), <u>heart</u> (emotions), <u>body</u>, and <u>soul</u> (will). These four parts are meant to interact as part of our relationships with God and neighbors. You may notice that these parts are separated by the horizontal and vertical elements of the cross. Without a healthy relationship with God and neighbors, we can become disconnected, dysfunctional, unhealthy, and in need of healing.

Some will argue that it is vanity to think of ourselves. Remember, everything must be in right relationship with God. We need to reflect on our gifts in humility so that we may be better stewards. We need to reflect on our sinful nature so that we may grow from vice to virtue. We need to reflect so as not to neglect or abuse an area of our personal being. However, it is for the right relationship with God that we must learn to love ourselves. God loves without condition, and we are to love our neighbors as ourselves and to grow from vice to virtue in both relationships. The measure of love is to love without measure. Again, these are by grace. Wherever grace is flowing, fruits will follow. Where fruits flow, we need to respond in gratitude, giving credit and praise to our wonderful God.

There is an outer circle as well. It passes over the arms and represents the Holy Spirit. The flow of divine love creates healing for the body, mind, heart, and our will. It maximizes our ability to let the gifts of the Holy Spirit flow. It leads to holiness. The letter of St. Paul to the Galatians sums it up:

> *If you are guided by the Spirit, you are not under the law. It is obvious what proceeds from the flesh: lewd conduct, impurity, licentiousness, idolatry, sorcery, hostilities, bickering, jealousy, outbursts of rage, selfish rivalries, dissensions, factions, envy, drunkenness, orgies, and the like. I warn you, as I have warned you before: those who do such things will not inherit the kingdom of God! In contrast, the fruit of the Spirit is love, joy, peace, patience, endurance, kindness, generosity, faith, mildness and chastity. Against such, there is no law.* (5:18-25)

If we stumble along the path as we do, there will be danger flags for the spiritually discerning pilgrim. If any part of our body is hurting or if any one of our three relationships is suffering, through prayerful reflection, we must respond. We must learn to do our part to engage in inner healing, as discussed in the next chapter, as soon as we become aware of damage.

How does one become holy? Is there a magic formula that we need to discover? The general nature of most people is to seek. We seek for different things in different ways. St. Augustine pointed out that our souls are created with an emptiness that only God can fill. One of the Church Fathers once said that theology is "faith seeking understanding." To grow in holiness takes grace, which is a free gift, but we must remember that we, too, have a role to play in this journey. These are a part of the good works. It takes discipline and, hence, discipleship.

I remember a lesson on spiritual growth that was the conclusion of a retreat that I was on. We were told that there are four things needed for spiritual growth: prayer, Bible study, the sacraments, and community, where you find prayer groups and service.

Prayer is a topic that has been written and talked about throughout history. For a novice, it can be overwhelming. Hopefully, children learn to pray in the family home. Prayer can be rote, creative, meditative, and contemplative. My biggest learning curve on prayer took place in prayer groups and related groups during my honeymoon stage. There is so much to learn about prayer, but the basic concept is that we dispose ourselves to God and enter into dialogue with Him. Spiritual growth is only as good as our prayer life. The ability and desire to pray is a gift, and the more we pray, the more we desire it and grow in it. The wider our experience of faith communities, the more fruitful is our growth on the spiritual path to holiness.

Bible study is a necessary element for growth. If you have never read the Bible, how do you begin? It is not easy without help. As I explained in my honeymoon stage, I was given a Bible on my 40th birthday with the recommendation of starting with the Gospel of St. John. I was starving for Scripture and for me it was an inspired start. Admittedly I had tried on other occasions but without success. We are exposed to Scripture whenever we gather in faith communities. As we learn new understandings of the Scripture passages, our desire to learn increases. So we grow through Scripture study by the grace of God and by our own efforts. I have been studying Scripture for almost 30 years, and I am still stimulated and fulfilled by the inspired Word of God. The growth never stops as long as we remain on the narrow path. At the end of the chapter, there is a quote from the Second Vatican Council on the reading of Scripture.

Sacramental life is another set of basics for spiritual growth. We are so blessed to have a Savior who understands our needs. He gave St. Peter the keys to the kingdom of Heaven and gave him authority to set up His Church. The Mass, including the sacrament of Holy Communion, evolved and is the central gift and source of grace that we have. God so loved us and wanted to stay with us. He initiated the sacrament of Holy Communion found in the Mass. He is eternally present in the tabernacles of the world, and the Mass is being celebrated somewhere in the world at all times. He is forever with us in that special sacrament of the altar.

The sacrament of Reconciliation is the partner to the sacrament of the Eucharist. It is by the grace of God that we grow in appreciation of it. Reconciliation is the emptying out of our sinful nature, whereas the Eucharist is the taking in of the divine nature. I will say more in the next chapter. In my opinion, if we understood and utilized this sacrament appropriately, we would not need any other forms of therapy.

The fourth component for spiritual growth is in community. We need each other for listening, sharing, consoling, positive affirmations, and correction. Previously, I mentioned a prayer group in my honeymoon stage. In it, we learned about different types of prayer, discerned from Scripture passages, sharing our understandings of the passages with lots of joyful praise and worship songs. There were testimonies. Fellowship and friendships evolved. Doors were opening, and I was growing and with each new lesson, I wanted more. A friend questioned my intensity with this new zeal. I responded as Thomas Merton once did: "This is Divine in origin and Divine in destiny." I'm still on the path

28 years later and still yearning to grow in my understanding of God and His awesome creation and Church teachings.

I previously mentioned prayer, Scripture study, and the four parts of the body. I have an example to make with reference to these. When praying meditatively or with Scripture, note how the four parts of the body enter into it. First, we need to dispose ourselves to God by <u>relaxing the body</u> and getting comfortable. Then we <u>empty our minds</u> of distracting thoughts. We read or listen to a passage and place ourselves into the environment by <u>using our intellect</u>. We revisit the passage, getting in touch with the characters in the Scripture. This interaction should <u>trigger the emotions</u> as we participate more fully in the reading. As we continue by talking to Jesus about this encounter, we may be challenged to <u>take action</u>, which now engages the will. Don't ever be discouraged if some of these elements are missing in your prayer time. It is your intention and desire that God loves. It is by His grace that we bear the fruits. It is when our relations with ourselves, our neighbors, and our God are healthy that we can continue on the narrow path to holiness.

Incidentally, here is a quote from the Second Vatican Council: Dogmatic Constitution on Divine Revelation:

> *The Sacred Scriptures contain the Word of God*
> *and since they are inspired, really are the Word of God…*

> *This sacred Synod urges all the Christian faithful*
> *to learn by frequent reading of the divine Scriptures*
> *the "excelling knowledge of Jesus Christ.*
> *For ignorance of the Scriptures is ignorance of Christ."*

> *Therefore, they should gladly put themselves*
> *in touch with the sacred text itself…*

And let them remember that prayer should accompany
the reading of Sacred Scripture,
so that God and man may talk together;
for "we speak to him when we pray;
we hear when we read the divine saying."

CHAPTER 21

Inner Healing

The word came to Jeremiah from the Lord: "Rise up, be off to the potter's house; there I will give you my message." I went down to the potter's house and there he was, working at the wheel. Whenever the object of clay which he was making turned out badly in his hand, he tried again, making of the clay another object of whatever sort he pleased. Then the word of the Lord came to me: "Can I not do to you, house of Israel, as the potter has done?" says the Lord. "Indeed like clay in the hands of the potter so are you in my hand O house of Israel." (Jeremiah18:1–6)

It was early in my honeymoon stage when I went to a workshop on "inner healing." It was a topic that I was hearing more and more about. I didn't know anything about inner healing, but I was certain that it didn't apply to me. I was naturally skeptical about going, but it was being offered by a sister whom I respected, so with the encouragement of a friend, I went.

One of the first exercises that we did was very revealing. We were to list our losses. In the 1980s I had experienced many losses. I had been divorced, experienced family break-up, suffered financial hardship, and struggled for child access. In the three years from 1985 to 1988, I had regular Sunday visitation plus many holidays with my two sons. Then my ex-wife, her new husband, and my two sons moved to Vancouver Island, which was a source of further sorrow and emotional trauma, especially after three years of extra bonding. My sons were nine and ten at that time. Also, I had lost a very good engineering job and, eventually, the loss of my engineering career. I had lost two properties in foreclosure and gone through the bankruptcy process. So, I had no problem in listing my losses. There were many, and they were highly stressful. It was a shock, however, to see the long list of things that I had survived in the 1980s. The resulting stress, according to the experts, was dangerously high. The prayer "Footsteps in the Sand" is very much a description of my relationship with the Lord at that time.

The second exercise of the workshop was very disturbing. We were to list the losses that we had been healed of. First of all, I didn't know what the question meant. What is healing? The question itself was very stressful. I couldn't identify one loss that I had been healed of! I came to realize that I needed a lot of healing. If I were to proceed, it was going to be a long, painful path. I knew that I did not like pain. I also knew that it was part of the journey that the Lord was leading me on. Others had told me to enjoy the honeymoon stage because it was only the beginning and there would be a lot of pain and healing as part of the spiritual journey.

The next part of the workshop was looking at the obstacles to healing. The first obstacle was denial. "There was no loss. It was meant to be." The second one followed the first. "It was meant to be, and something better will come along as a replacement." I was able to identify completely. It seemed to me that somebody was stripping me of my protective shelter called "denial." I couldn't stay in hiding, where I felt both safe yet miserable at the same time. I knew that what was presented to me that day was the truth. Like any truth, I can remember it as if it had just occurred, but in reality, it was over 27 years ago. It was a tough pill to swallow. I went home after the workshop and did what I quite often do when I'm dealing with stress. I took a long nap.

So, how does healing take place? The best answer is it requires faith. The Lord will lead you to where he wants you to go. Thomas was lacking in faith when the other apostles told him that Jesus had appeared to them. He replied that he would not believe until he could touch and see the nail marks and the hole in the side of Jesus. When Jesus appeared again to the apostles, this time, Thomas was with them. He was healed instantly of his disbelief! He proclaimed, "My Lord and my God" (John 20:28).

I can identify with Thomas. When Jesus appeared to me during the night that I was "born again," I felt all the love, mercy, and forgiveness that the apostles had felt. After all, they had all abandoned him, and so had I on too many occasions. Jesus came to invite me to follow him. I'm still trying to discern the meaning of that divine invitation. I know it was divine because it still brings me peace and joy when I remember it. If tears and sobbing are signs of healing, then I received tremendous healing that night. I cried while kneeling by my bedside, reciting repeatedly the Act of Contrition until, eventually, I fell asleep.

I mentioned previously my crying at the Live-In and my pilgrimage to Medjugorje. I believe that the healing from these two events was divine. I had not gone for any psychological therapy for anything in my dark times in the 1980s, and yet the Lord had rescued me and started healing me in the safe environment of a faith community with many other healing souls on the same journey. A missionary once told me that the Church is not a museum of saints, but a hospital of sinners. The other souls provided me with much comfort and encouragement.

When Jesus brought Lazarus back to life, he called him out of the tomb and had others unbind him. Does this mean that Jesus wants us to unbind each other? The 12-step program and its many participants would agree. Prayer groups who pray for healing would agree. Anyone who has prayed for someone else's healing and has had prayers answered would agree. I, too, had many healing experiences in my faith community. I had been involved in charismatic prayer groups, 12-step workshops, spiritual exercises, and other healing workshops in the early 1990s. I previously mentioned, as a result of one of my workshops, healing from my dreams.

I'm convinced, however, that the greatest form of healing comes in the sacrament of Reconciliation. This sacrament was instituted during the first appearance to the apostles when Thomas was absent. *"Then he breathed on them and said, 'Receive the Holy Spirit. If you forgive the sins of men, they are forgiven them; if you hold them bound they are held bound'"* (John 20: 22–23).

My first experience of healing from Confession was just prior to my encounter with Jesus on that special night. The priest had asked me to pray on the Scripture passage when the Good Shepherd set out to find the lost sheep (Matthew 18:10–14). He asked me to see myself as the lost sheep and that Jesus was bringing me back to the fold. I experienced a feeling of being safe, loved, wanted, and valued. It was also my first experience of placing myself in a Scripture passage instead of just reading it as a storybook. It was an experience of divine revelation from praying with Scripture. The Bible is a powerful instrument in developing a personal relationship with Jesus, but somehow, it is the work of the Holy Spirit to make the Word come alive.

When I began going to the University of Calgary Catholic Community in 1988, the priest, Fr. Dave, was able to capture my intellect as no other priest had done before. I was starving for the Word of God because this was just after I had been "born again." His strengths were in preaching and in talking about healing. Healing at that time was still just a word that I had not connected to my life. He emphasized that we need to name it, claim it, embrace it, and let it go. He would recommend as a Lenten project to find an imperfection in our lives and to deal with it in the forty days prior to Easter but to leave it at the foot of the cross on Good Friday.

In order to talk the talk, you have to walk the walk. Yes, I have had some powerful healing experiences. In the 1980s I was in a very dysfunctional relationship with a drinking companion, and I learned from the school of hard knocks what relationships should not be. I was very vulnerable and weak from all the stress I had in my dark years, and so I remained in the relationship despite how obvious it was that it was not going anywhere. After being "born again," she offered me a drink of wine, which she had done many times before. This time, I refused. She, however, was going to have one anyway without me. I noticed how one drink of wine changed her speech and, indeed, her personality. I was able to walk away from her this time, graciously, and stay away from her, something I had wanted to do and had tried to do on several occasions. Each time, feelings of guilt would draw me back into more dysfunctional interactions with her. It seems to me that it was an instantaneous change within me. I was able to say no to alcohol from that moment on. I had been in that relationship for seven years, and in an instant, I was free and healed! I now hate what alcohol does to people, although for too many years, I was a party animal. This event took place after I had been to Medjugorje. It had been a miraculous healing! Thank you, Jesus !

Recently, our parish priest asked if any of us had ever missed a doctor's appointment. People rarely miss doctor's appointments, yet missing Mass on Sunday is hardly given a second thought. Going to Confession has taken a big backslide in recent years. Healing, along with teaching and preaching, was one of Christ's greatest gifts, and He is still waiting to heal us! I have tried psychological and psychiatric therapy in a variety of ways, both individually and in groups. They have all cost some money but given small satisfaction. There is no comparison to the peace of Christ after Reconciliation! After all, it is the Creator of the universe and of all eternity who is embracing us in that wonderful underused sacrament. Thank you, Jesus!

The topic of the rosary could be included almost anywhere in my book. It is a tool of intercessory prayer, discernment, healing, meditation, reflection, and much more. It is historically fascinating. The prayers in monasteries changed from 150 psalms to 150 recitations of the Hail Mary. It is a central theme in the Marian apparitions. The stories and witnessing of miracles connected to the rosary are astronomical. The narrow path to holiness is as much about healing as it is about going from vice to virtue.

I find it noteworthy that the intentions of the rosary are centered on the virtues. In reviewing the rosary, there are four sets of mysteries with five decades in each set. The first set consists of the joyful mysteries, with the intentions of humility, charity towards neighbors, poverty of spirit, obedience, and piety. The second set is that of the sorrowful mysteries, with intentions of true contrition, purity, fortification, patience, and final perseverance. The third set consists of the glorious mysteries, with intentions of faith, hope, charity, eternal salvation, and a devotion to Mary. The latest set was requested by Pope John Paul II. They are called the luminous mysteries, and their intentions are of submission to God's will, devotion to Mary, conversion, fear of God, and thanksgiving to God. So, if prayer is central to staying on the narrow path, then how much more powerful is prayer for virtue through the prayer of the rosary in which Mother Mary is pleading for us to her son Jesus!

The rosary has consistently been a part of my daily devotion for 30 years. I never tire of it. There have been many blessings resulting from praying the rosary. It has consistently provided me with peace in my heart. I have had many inspired ideas for the writing of this book while praying the rosary. Pray, write, pray, revise. Just as the potter refines the clay, so the Spirit refines my writing, and so does He refine my soul in divine healing as I travel on the journey. Thank you, Lord, for your many spiritual gifts!

As a matter of fact, I need to tell of a recent miracle. A friend of mine sent me an email with some of her promotional YouTube material attached. I opened one that appealed to me regarding Fatima and watched it. I noticed a picture in the video. It seemed to complement the cover page for this book, which I had only started to design. After a couple of days of thought, I went back to the picture, captured it on my iPhone, and had it developed.

I thanked my friend for her email and the YouTube video that I had received. She informed me that she had not sent me any videos about Fatima. I double-checked my email; it was still present. In disbelief, I went to her place, and we viewed her email. All of her promotional YouTube videos were still attached, but there was no evidence of the picture that I had received! I call this a miracle, and I'm convinced that it is

God's way of directing me with my back page. After all, I had made this an intention earlier! I call it my miracle picture!

And recently, I have had another inspiration relating to healing. I am not an authority, only God is, so when I am given an inspired thought, I believe I must share. So, here it is. There are three spiritual parts to healing. They are love, mercy, and forgiveness.

In 1989, I started crying at my Live-In, in Medjugorje, and during Mass. I experienced tears, sobbing, and crying for most of the year, and it was always accompanied by the presence of the peace that only Christ can give. I can only explain it as an outpouring of <u>God's love.</u> I don't know what I was being healed of, but it was overwhelming. Of course, my separation from God was mortally serious until He invited me to follow Him. So, in faith, I simply know that God was healing me! *"Love, then consists in this: not that we have loved God, but that He has loved us and has sent His only Son as an offering for our sins"* (1 John 4:10).

The second component of healing is <u>mercy.</u> As compared to grace, which is an unconditional gift from God that is not earned nor expected, mercy is the absence of a punishment that we think we have somehow deserved. A good example can be found in John 8, in which an adulteress woman is brought before Jesus and the Pharisees are trying to trap Jesus. They expect Him to condemn her. As related in verse 7: "He said to them, 'Let the man among you that has no sin be the first to cast a stone at her.'" They all left her until she was alone with Jesus, who said, "Nor do I condemn you. You may go. But from now on, avoid this sin" (v. 11).

As stated earlier, after my divorce, I thought I was damned to eternal hellfire. When I was given my annulment, the greatest load I have ever carried was removed from my shoulders. It was a total act of mercy that contributed to much healing from my past. Mercy is the removal of an expected punishment.

The third component in healing is <u>forgiveness</u>. Forgiveness has many steps, and not being a professional, I will express only my beliefs based on my experience. The best prescription I can suggest is a sincere confession in the sacrament of Reconciliation. When I confess, I am putting myself into the presence of Christ, where he is waiting for me so that my friendship with Him can be continued. As a sinner, I turn away from Him, and He waits for me to turn back to Him. The priest is an ordained representative of the Church, and he absolves me from my sins. What an awesome sacrament instituted by Christ to give us grace!

The most important part of forgiveness is <u>self-forgiveness.</u> When I accept Jesus completely as my Lord and Savior, and when I participate in the sacrament of Reconciliation, self-forgiveness becomes much easier. I believe that the factors of love, mercy, and forgiveness play a major role in healing. I also believe that the process of healing is ongoing and never complete. Hence the need for daily self-examination!

CHAPTER 22

Self-Examination

> *Two men went up to the temple to pray; one was a Pharisee and the other a tax collector. The Pharisee with head unbowed prayed in this fashion: "I give you thanks, O God, that I am not like the rest of men-grasping, crooked, adulterous-or even like this tax collector. I fast twice a week. I pay tithes on all I possess." The other man, however, kept his distance, not even daring to raise his eyes to heaven. All he did was beat his breast and say, "O God be merciful to me a sinner." Believe me, this man went home justified but the other did not.*

> (Luke 18:10–13)

The difference between a <u>hypocrite</u> and a <u>sinner</u> is that a hypocrite doesn't accept being a sinner. He does not see the hypocrisy in his dealings with others. He has a double standard. Actions that are wrong for others are acceptable to him. The sinner sees his own hypocrisy and acknowledges his human imperfection. The hypocrite, being blind, has no choice. He is locked into a pattern and will continue in his ways. The sinner, unlike the Pharisee, sees his own hypocrisy and wishes to make corrections.

The <u>sinner</u> can make choices that will lead him to <u>sainthood.</u> He must first become resolved to make an honest attempt to change his direction. He must also make amends where it is possible. If he has caused damage in a relationship, he must seek reconciliation and forgiveness with a new understanding of the adjusted roles in the relationship. Transformation is about getting on the path to holiness. He can choose to pursue holiness. After all, saints were first sinners, but they confessed and did much work to perfect their human condition. The Church is not a museum of saints, but a hospital of sinners. Sainthood is a process, one that never ends until perfection is achieved. It is the work of the pilgrim on the spiritual journey to holiness.

The Catholic Catechism,1030, states: *"All who die in God's grace and friendship, but still imperfectly purified, are indeed assured of their eternal salvation; but after death they undergo purification, so as to achieve the holiness necessary to enter the joy of heaven."* Scriptures support this claim. Revelations 21:27 says: *"Nothing unclean can enter heaven."* Catholics have given the name "Purgatory" to this place of purging. Is it possible that we can minimize or eliminate our time in Purgatory by the quality of our discipleship? I would much rather do as much as I can while on earth than wait to find out what Purgatory is like!

Daily reflection is, therefore, a necessary tool for the journey. Without reflection, a sinful action can so easily be repeated, and the conscience can be numbed. In my own experience, I know that repetition leads to pacifying our conscience. Once a pattern, it takes the path of least resistance until there is no longer any resistance and Satan has the victory. He can now lead us to more severe sins and develop even more mortal patterns. It is through prayerful reflection that we can see our daily shortcomings. A simple error is much easier to correct than a large one. After all, "a stitch in time saves nine."

> *Woe to you, scribes and pharisees, hypocrites! For you clean the outside of the cup and of the plate, but inside they are full of greed and self-indulgence. You blind Pharisee! First clean the inside of the cup, so that the outside also may become clean.*

(Matthew 23:23–26)

The above passage from Matthew was part of the daily readings for the Mass of Aug. 22, 2016, which I had attended. I woke up the next morning feeling very desolate. I sensed that spiritually, I was hurting. I feel that way sometimes when I have hurt someone in a relationship, but I couldn't think of anyone that I had wronged. So, I prayed the rosary and again went over the reading from the day before. I felt like those hypocrites, but why? After all, I had just been to Confession during the pilgrimage at Rama to celebrate the feast of the Assumption of our Lady into Heaven. I had prayed the rosary, done the Stations of the Cross and been very prayerful. I started to realize that I was like the Pharisees. I was doing everything right and, furthermore, feeling self-righteous about it. I was starting to realize that I am sometimes judgmental towards others who appear to be weak in practicing their faith. I was forgetting that I have no right to judge and my role is to pray for them and to strengthen them. Small scales had been removed from my eyes, and I could see more clearly again. I would confess at my earliest convenience. Coincidentally, Aug 22 is the feast day of Mary's Queenship of the Heavens. Mother Mary was scolding me about my attitudes to her other children. I was being disciplined, taught, and healed by the Mother of God on her feast day!

In the study of the Spiritual Exercises, there are two opposite movements. When we are moving closer to God, we experience consolation, which, in simplest terms, is a feeling of peace. When we are moving away from God, we experience desolation. In spiritual discernment, we are taught to react accordingly, especially from desolation. When in desolation, continue to practice all regular good works even if the feeling is absent. We are being weaned off the feeling that is so rewarding, but it is necessary in order to make us stronger.

Also in the Study of the Exercises, we develop the discipline of the Daily Examen. We remember the events of the day and discern how God was actively present to us. It might be a time to recognize our gifts and to express gratitude. Or perhaps we were challenged to make a change or to initiate action. Regardless, the discipline develops a deeper understanding of how God relates to us and strengthens our ability to respond to Him. Is there a better way of ending the day than by talking to God as a personal friend?

> *A clean heart create for me, O God, and a steadfast spirit renew within me.*

> (Psalm 51:12)

CHAPTER 23

On Evangelization

> *On the last and greatest day of the festival, Jesus stood up and cried out: "If anyone thirsts, let him come to me; let him drink who believes in me." Scripture has it: "From within him rivers of living water shall flow."*

(John 7:37–38)

I was a sponsor in the RCIA (Rite of the Christian Initiation for Adults) program in Calgary in 1991, and in 1992, I was invited to join the leadership team at St. Pius X, which I enjoyed until 1995. It was an interesting time because there had been ongoing discussions on the topic of evangelizing and catechizing. Prior to that time, most parishes offered RCIA as an informational program based on catechizing. The target date was the Easter Vigil, when the candidates would be fully accepted into the Church with Baptism, if unbaptized, First Communion, and Confirmation. Those who were curious, the inquirers, would begin with everyone else. The meetings had a classroom environment.

Some of the leaders of RCIA had noticed that some candidates fell away after being initiated. As in any discussion, there are always a variety of factors. One factor was emphasized and agreed upon: those people had not been evangelized. As a new team member, I was privileged to enter at the brainstorming level of discernment on altering the program. The first step is to make it a process and not a program, and it begins at the inquiry stage, where inquirers get to know Jesus as their personal Savior. This happens when people are gathered and telling their stories of their personal encounters with Christ. The meetings are not information based and must have a different setting than the rest of the program. Candidates, sponsors, and others share and discuss their personal stories. Having a charismatic background and prayer group experience, I had found my niche. Talking about the works and wonders of Jesus is always exciting, if not infectious. People were being evangelized and were happy to remain in the inquiry stage. In a healthy parish, there is a flow of new people coming in. It was only after the inquirers were satisfied and hopefully converted that they entered into the catechumenate through the Rite of Acceptance. There were other changes in the delivery of the program to emphasize evangelizing in order to create desire for continued learning of our beautiful faith. The major shift was to change the classroom environment from delivery of information to a discussion-based environment where everyone's input contributed to communal learning. It became formational rather than informational. Lectio Divina was included in this change of delivery.

Evangelization is a goal of our modern Church. In the early 1990s, I was present at a charismatic conference, and I heard a preaching on evangelizing. I have never forgotten it. In John 4:4–41, we see Jesus meeting the Samaritan woman at the well. We also see her reaction after her encounter with Him. The priest used the experience of the woman at the well as an outline for evangelizing. She was evangelized and then took her turn to evangelize. There are four main points that can be taken from her story and analyzed. The woman obviously was shocked that Jesus would speak to her. In verse 9, The Samaritan woman says to Him, *"You are a Jew. How can you ask me, a Samaritan and a woman, for a drink?"*

The first point is to have a need for help. The reading reveals a series of broken relationships from her past. Jesus knew her pain, and in verse 18, he replies, *"The fact is you have had five husbands, and the man you are living with is not your husband."* It would appear obvious that this poor woman had experienced many hardships. Have you ever had a troubling situation that you could have used some help with?

The second step is to be openly seeking. She had a curiosity about whether to worship on the mountain or in Jerusalem. She believed that *"there was a Messiah coming"* (v. 25) and that when He came, He would tell her everything. In one short conversation, she revealed her curious, seeking mind. Jesus knew everything. He even told her that *"the man she was living with was not her husband."* Could you turn to Jesus and, in prayer, ask for help? Are you wanting a personal relationship with Jesus Christ?

The third step is to recognize Him and to accept Jesus Christ as your personal Savior. He told her that He was the living water, and she believed that she had encountered the Messiah. In verse 15, she asks for the living water that will provide eternal life. How has Christ spoken to you today? Are you waiting and watching for Him so that you too can talk to Him as your personal Savior?

What was her reaction? She told her story, which is the last or fourth step. *"She went off into the town. She said to the people: Come and see someone who told me everything I ever did! Could this not be the Messiah"* (v. 28–29). *"Many Samaritans from that town believed in Him on the strength of the woman's word of testimony"* (v. 39). I would like to think that her testimony was the beginning of her ministry as an evangelist.

To summarize, the four steps, as discussed above, are to have a need, to be seeking, to recognize and accept Christ as your personal Savior when you encounter Him, and to tell the story. Who can tell the story? We all have a story. Remember the first section of my book?

I was in so much pain that I didn't even realize that I was the lost sheep. I didn't know that I needed healing, and yet I was seeking. I had accepted false solutions (more wine and more of a dysfunctional relationship), which lasted far too long. Yet I was always in His hands. He knew the best timing to appear to me. And when He did, I was ready. I have been telling my story ever since.

Do you have a story? If you have experienced pain, suffering, or confusion, you have a need. *"Come to me, all you who are weary and find life burdensome and I will refresh you"* (Matthew 11:28). If you turn to prayer, you are seeking. If your situation has been *lightened through prayer*, give credit to God for all good things that come from Him. Then tell your story. In telling your story, it is necessary to give credit, thanks, and glory to God in humility. In other words, you need to have had a personal encounter with Jesus, and you must have accepted Him as your personal Lord and Savior. If you take any credit, you are falling into pride. Any special quality that you have used to solve your problem is a gift. It is the Giver, not the gift, that you need to acknowledge! Now you can tell your story, giving Christ all the glory. Your evangelizing is in living the Gospel but is completed in telling your story and giving God the glory.

"What we have seen and heard we proclaim in turn to you so that you may share life with us. This fellowship of ours is with

the Father and with His Son, Jesus Christ" (1 John 1:3). This is how much of the evangelizing was done in the early Church.

In Revelations 12, there is a battle between a woman and the dragon. Verses 10–11 say: *"Now have salvation and power come . . . They defeated him by the blood of the Lamb and <u>by the power of His testimony.</u>"* I believe that as Christians, we must tell our story. In evangelizing, we must not only talk the talk, but walk the walk. As Jesus ascended into Heaven, He said, *"Go into the world and proclaim the good news to all creation"* (Mark 6:15). Evangelizing is far more effective when accompanied by a successful testimonial story. I remember a friend saying: "Before the imperative, there is a narrative." Make it your story of salvation as granted by Jesus Christ. All glory be to the Father, the Son, and the Holy Spirit. Amen.